Pathfinder® Guides

Hampshire

Walks

Fully revised by
David Foster

Acknowledgements
This new edition has been extensively re-written to reflect the creation of the South Downs National Park, and includes 20 new or substantially adapted routes. Nevertheless, I have drawn on the work of Jenny Plucknett and Nick Channer, as well as John Cawley of the Eastleigh Ramblers, all of whom contributed to earlier editions of this book.

Text:	David Foster
Photography:	Crimson Publishing, Jenny Plucknett, David Foster, Kevin Freeborn
Editorial:	Ark Creative (UK) Ltd
Design:	Ark Creative (UK) Ltd

ISBN: 978-1-85458-552-3

While every care has been taken to ensure the accuracy of the route directions, the publishers cannot accept responsibility for errors or omissions, or for changes in details given. The countryside is not static: hedges and fences can be removed, field boundaries can alter, footpaths can be rerouted and changes in ownership can result in the closure or diversion of some concessionary paths. Also, paths that are easy and pleasant for walking in fine conditions may become slippery, muddy and difficult in wet weather, while stepping stones across rivers and streams may become impassable.

If you find an inaccuracy in either the text or maps, please write to Crimson Publishing at the address below.

First published 1993 by Jarrold Publishing
Revised and reprinted 1996, 2000, 2003, 2006, 2008, 2010.

Printed in Singapore. 10/10

This edition first published in Great Britain 2010 by Crimson Publishing, a division of:
Crimson Business Ltd,
Westminster House, Kew Road, Richmond, Surrey, TW9 2ND

www.totalwalking.co.uk

A catalogue record for this book is available from the British library.

Front cover: East Meon church from Small Down
Previous page: Beaulieu Palace House

Contents

Approximate walk times

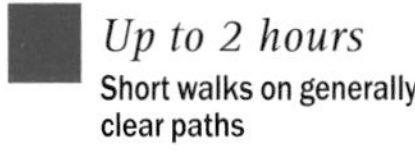
Up to 2 hours
Short walks on generally clear paths

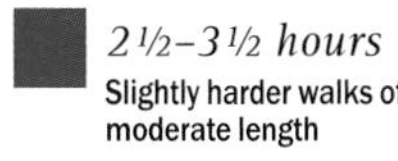
2½–3½ hours
Slightly harder walks of moderate length

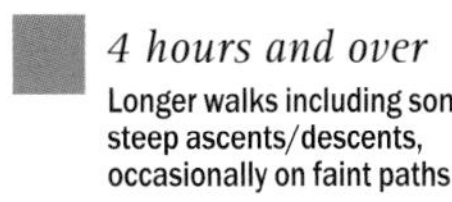
4 hours and over
Longer walks including some steep ascents/descents, occasionally on faint paths

The walk times are provided as a guide only and are calculated using an average walking speed of 2½mph (4km/h), adding one minute for each 10m (33ft) of ascent, and then rounding the result to the nearest half hour.

Keymap

SCALE 1:333 333 or 1 INCH to about 5¼ MILES *1CM to 3.3KM*

0 2 4 6 8 10 KILOMETRES 15

0 2 4 6 MILES 8 10

SPOT HEIGHTS SHOWN IN METRES

Keymap

BASINGSTOKE
Tadley
Pamber Heath
Silchester
Bramley
Sherfield on Loddon
Hook
Old Basing
Chineham
Overton
Oakley
Kingsclere
Ramsdell
Wolverton
Hartley Wintney
Crowthorne
Sandhurst
Yateley
FARNBOROUGH
FLEET
ALDERSHOT
Odiham
North Warnborough
Crookham Village
Crondall
FARNHAM
Bentley
Dippenhall
Wrecclesham
Rowledge
Frensham
Hale
Weybourne
Runfold
Long Sutton
Upton Grey
Ellisfield
Herriard
Dummer
Popham
Micheldever
Preston Candover
Alton
Holybourne
Four Marks
Ropley
New Alresford
Bishop's Sutton
Chawton
Selborne
Kingsley
BORDON
Headley
Lindford
Liphook
Liss
Greatham
PETERSFIELD
Steep
Rake
Milland
MIDHURST
Rogate
West Meon
East Meon
Warnford
Exton
Corhampton
Meonstoke
Droxford
Bishop's Waltham
Clanfield
Catherington
HORNDEAN
Cowplain
Waterlooville
Purbrook
HAVANT
EMSWORTH
Southbourne
Bosham
CHICHESTER
Wickham
FAREHAM
Portchester
Gosport
PORTSMOUTH
Southsea
Portsea Island
Hayling Island
South Hayling
Stubbington
Lee-on-the-Solent
Hill Head
Botley
Selsey
Selsey Bill
East Wittering
Sidlesham
Ryde
East Cowes
Whippingham
Spithead
Cheriton
Bramdean
Hinton Ampner
Tichborne
Chilcomb
Owslebury
Upham
Swanmore
Shirrell Heath
Rowlands Castle
Forest of Bere
Compton
West Marden
Harting
M3
M27
A3(M)
A31
A32
A272
A339

At-a-glance

Walk	Page	Start	Nat. Grid Reference	Distance	Time	Height Gain
Ashmansworth and Crux Easton	18	Ashmansworth	SU 415574	3 miles (5km)	1½ hrs	280ft (85m)
Bentley and the Hampshire Downs	81	Bentley	SU 783439	9¼ miles (15km)	4½ hrs	740ft (225m)
Bishop's Dyke, New Forest	12	Pig Bush, off the B3056	SU 362050	2¼ miles (3.8km)	1 hr	100ft (30m)
Brockenhurst Park and Roydon Woods	47	Brockenhurst	SU 315025	5¼ miles (8.3km)	2½ hrs	345ft (105m)
Chalk streams at Fullerton	35	West Down, near Fullerton	SU 383389	4½ miles (7.3km)	2½ hrs	310ft (95m)
Cheriton & Hinton Ampner	30	Cheriton	SU 582284	4½ miles (7.4km)	2 hrs	345ft (105m)
Chilcomb and the South Downs	53	Cheesefoot Head on the A272	SU 529277	6¼ miles (10km)	3 hrs	690ft (210m)
Coasting around Keyhaven	69	Keyhaven	SZ 306914	7¼ miles (11.8km)	4 hrs	n/a
Denmead and the cradle of cricket	77	Denmead	SU 659120	9 miles (14.5km)	4 hrs	720ft (220m)
East Meon and the Downs	38	East Meon	SU 677222	4¾ miles (7.8km)	2½ hrs	605ft (185m)
Fritham and Ashley Walk	44	Fritham	SU 231141	5¼ miles (8.5km)	2½ hrs	310ft (95m)
Hillhead and Titchfield	56	Hillhead Harbour	SU 535023	6½ miles (10.5km)	3 hrs	n/a
Holmsley's old railway and Whitten Pond	22	Holmsley	SU 222011	4 miles (6.5km)	2 hrs	115ft (35m)
Itchen Abbas & the water babies	62	Micheldever Wood	SU 529362	6½ miles (10.5km)	3 hrs	490ft (150m)
Kingsclere and Watership Down	88	Kingsclere	SU 526586	10¼ miles (16.5km)	5 hrs	935ft (285m)
Meon Valley rails and trails	73	Beacon Hill, near Meonstoke	SU 598227	7¾ miles (12.5km)	4 hrs	720ft (220m)
New Forest snapshot	14	Millyford Bridge	SU 267079	2¾ miles (4.5km)	1½ hrs	130ft (40m)
Odiham and the Basingstoke Canal	28	Odiham Wharf	SU 747516	4½ miles (7.3km)	2 hrs	150ft (45m)
Queen Elizabeth Country Park	50	Off the A3 south of Petersfield	SU 718185	5½ miles (9km)	3 hrs	1,035ft (315m)
Rockbourne and Breamore	65	Rockbourne	SU 113182	7 miles (11.3km)	3½ hrs	690ft (210m)
Selborne and Noar Hill	32	Selborne	SU 742335	4¼ miles (7km)	2½ hrs	590ft (180m)
Silchester's Roman town	26	Silchester	SU 635629	4 miles (6.5km)	2 hrs	280ft (85m)
Standing Hat, New Forest	41	Brockenhurst	SU 314036	5 miles (8km)	2½ hrs	150ft (45m)
Stockbridge and Danebury Hill	84	Stockbridge	SU 355351	10 miles (16km)	4½ hrs	310ft (95m)
Test Valley rails and trails	59	Horsebridge	SU 344304	6½ miles (10.5km)	3 hrs	330ft (100m)
The Itchen Valley	20	Between Easton and Avington	SU 528320	3½ miles (5.5km)	1½ hrs	180ft (55m)
Warsash waterside and woodland	24	Warsash	SU 489062	4 miles (6.3km)	2 hrs	130ft (40m)
Winchester's water meadows	16	Garnier Road, Winchester	SU 483280	3 miles (5km)	1½ hrs	n/a

Comments

Starting from Hampshire's highest village, this route offers great views of Highclere Castle. You'll also visit an intriguing wind engine, while a delightful little Georgian church lies just yards off the route.

This walk heads out into the surprisingly remote countryside north of Bentley, known for its starring role in Radio 4's series *The Village*. Bentley also has links with the Scout movement.

A short walk that encompasses typical New Forest streams, heathland and ancient woodland. As a bonus, duckboards lead you easily across a wetland area with a fascinating past.

Lots of interest on this woodland walk, which includes the oldest church in the New Forest with its notable churchyard memorials. Look out, too, for the former home of the author W H Hudson.

A varied route that circles the confluence of two chalk streams and crosses the steep watershed between them. The walk includes a nature reserve, an abandoned railway, and the enchanting Fullerton Mill.

In 1644, Cheriton was the scene of a decisive Civil War battle. This walk offers views of the battlefield before tracking the boundary of the National Trust's charming Hinton Ampner estate.

Enjoy big skies and dramatic views at the western end of the South Downs National Park. The route follows the South Downs Way through the secluded village of Chilcomb.

A versatile route in two distinct sections, this walk blends country tracks with exposed coastal paths. There are stunning views, a Tudor castle, and an optional ferry trip that's great for children.

Field paths and tracks lead you on an enjoyable pilgrimage to the isolated Hampshire pub where the laws of cricket were first established more than 200 years ago.

This varied route includes a significant stretch of the South Downs Way National Trail. Beginning and ending along farmland paths, the walk climbs onto the Downs for spectacular views.

Combining both woods and heaths, this relatively remote route also skirts the edge of an important wartime bombing range. Do not miss the iconic Royal Oak pub near the start of your walk.

Combining coast and country, the route follows a disused 17th-century canal to Titchfield village. Turning south along farm tracks, the walk ends with a bracing stretch along the cliffs to Meon Shore.

The ponds and heaths south of Burley are the focus of this attractive route, which includes a stretch of abandoned railway line. There's a welcome refreshment stop in a converted old station.

With the ghosts of Hampshire's early cricketers for company, this route crosses the high chalk downs to visit the Itchen valley pub where Charles Kingsley wrote much of his classic fable *The Water Babies*.

Traverse the lonely hills south of Kingsclere to reach Watership Down, immortalised in Richard Adams' heroic fable. Your route returns past the home of Andrew Lloyd-Webber at Sydmonton.

The Meon Valley railway trail forms the backbone of a route that also includes parts of the South Downs Way. Take a break in West Meon – and do not miss the church that crossed the Atlantic!

One of the New Forest's oldest trees is the highlight to this short woodland walk, which also takes you to a former wartime encampment and the New Forest Reptile Centre.

The appealing market town of Odiham is the focus of a walk beside the quiet waters of the Basingstoke Canal. The route also passes the 13th-century ruins of Odiham Castle.

Explore the two faces of Queen Elizabeth Country Park. There's a gentle woodland loop, and a stiff climb up the grassy slopes of Butser Hill to the highest point on the South Downs.

Field paths and woodland tracks link the seasonal attractions of Rockbourne Roman villa and the Elizabethan manor house at Breamore. This walk offers the potential for a full day out.

Explore the beechwoods and fields around Selborne, immortalised by the 18th-century naturalist Gilbert White. Leave time to visit his former home, now a museum in the heart of the village.

After exploring the wooded farmland close to Hampshire's northern border, this walk reaches its climax with a circuit of the mysterious remains of the Roman town of Calleva Atrebatum.

A walk for all seasons. Shady in summer, this enjoyable woodland walk offers some appealing informal picnic stops. It makes use of all-weather gravel tracks that are ideal when other areas lie waterlogged.

From the home of fly fishing to an iconic Iron Age hill fort, this route follows country tracks and an abandoned railway line beside the famous River Test.

After following an old railway beside the River Test, the walk joins the Clarendon Way towards Broughton. Field paths and farm tracks lead you back past the former Horsebridge railway station.

The film location at Avington Park and an unrestored Georgian church are features of this attractive route, which meanders through the valley of one of Hampshire's most famous fishing rivers.

A varied walk that sets off beside the famous River Hamble, then turns inland through an unusual woodland park. Leave time for the optional ferry trip to Hamble-le-Rice.

This quiet waterside stroll explores the Itchen Navigation and Britain's oldest almshouses, whilst a short diversion will take you to the historic attractions of central Winchester.

Introduction to Hampshire

From its chalk stream valleys and high downlands to its bluebell woods and wide purple heaths, Hampshire's varied landscapes make ideal walking country. As you might expect, Hampshire offers a profusion of thatched villages and picturesque country pubs. More surprisingly, perhaps, you'll discover plenty of remote countryside within 70 miles of London where you can walk all day and scarcely see a soul.

But don't just take my word for it – the Government recently gave its seal of approval to Hampshire's remarkable scenery by creating two 21st-century National Parks. As we'll explore in a moment, the South Downs and the New Forest are, quite literally, as different as chalk from cheese, yet they both share the outstanding qualities that put them among Britain's finest landscapes.

For all that, it would be wrong to ignore Hampshire's wider countryside, which encompasses the Test Valley, the Downs north of Andover, and Winchester's water meadows. Much of the county's coastline has now been developed, yet even here experienced walkers can still find solitude on lonely shores with stunning views to the Isle of Wight. The walks in this book will take you to prehistoric and Roman sites, as well as exploring cultural locations and varied aspects of the county's more recent heritage.

Hampshire's history – ancient and modern

Daily life has endured in Hampshire for many thousands of years, and our forebears have left earthworks like the Iron Age strongholds at Danebury and St Catherine's Hill near Winchester. The Romans, too, left their mark in places as diverse as Silchester and Rockbourne, though the county's identity still lay in the future. Until modern times it was known as the 'County of Southampton', a name that comes from the Saxon words 'ham', or land by a river, and 'tun', meaning a village.

Yet it was not in Southampton, but in Winchester that King Alfred made his capital, and his commanding statue in Broadway still dominates the lower part of the city. Later, in the 14th century, William of Wykeham (Bishop of Winchester) transformed the interior of his great Norman cathedral and founded Winchester College, which remains England's oldest public school.

Hampshire's salt industry was already thriving in William's time, leaving behind the shallow lagoons and salt dock that you'll see on the coast between Keyhaven and Pennington. Even before the Industrial Revolution, new transport routes began to penetrate Hampshire's rural heart. You can still walk the length of a 17th-century waterway from

The Balmer Lawn Hotel at Brockenhurst – the D-Day landings HQ

the Solent to Titchfield, or stroll inland beside its more recent cousin, the Basingstoke Canal. The railways came later still, and some of the lines that were abandoned in the 20th century have now been converted into walking trails through Britain's newest National Parks.

A new generation of National Parks

Designated as a National Park in 2006, the New Forest lies almost wholly within Hampshire. Yet much of its character dates back to 1079, when William the Conqueror declared the Forest a royal hunting park. William established the right of 'commoners' to graze their animals in his royal playground, so creating the wide purple heaths where their ponies and cattle still thrive to this day.

In contrast, the large wooded 'inclosures' were established in Tudor times, reflecting the Royal Navy's growing appetite for shipbuilding timber. Yet this was a policy for the long term – the first naval timber was not felled until 1611, and warships were built locally at Buckler's Hard until the early years of the 19th century.

Today, up to 25 million people use the New Forest every year for leisure and recreation. Over 100 miles of off-road tracks wind through its woods and heaths, which are internationally important for wildlife. You might struggle to see the shy little Dartford warbler, but buzzards, kestrels and sparrowhawks are common sights throughout the year. The sandy heaths are home to all six of Britain's native reptiles including rare smooth snakes and sand lizards, whilst the wetter parts support unusual plants like sundew, marsh gentian and bog asphodel.

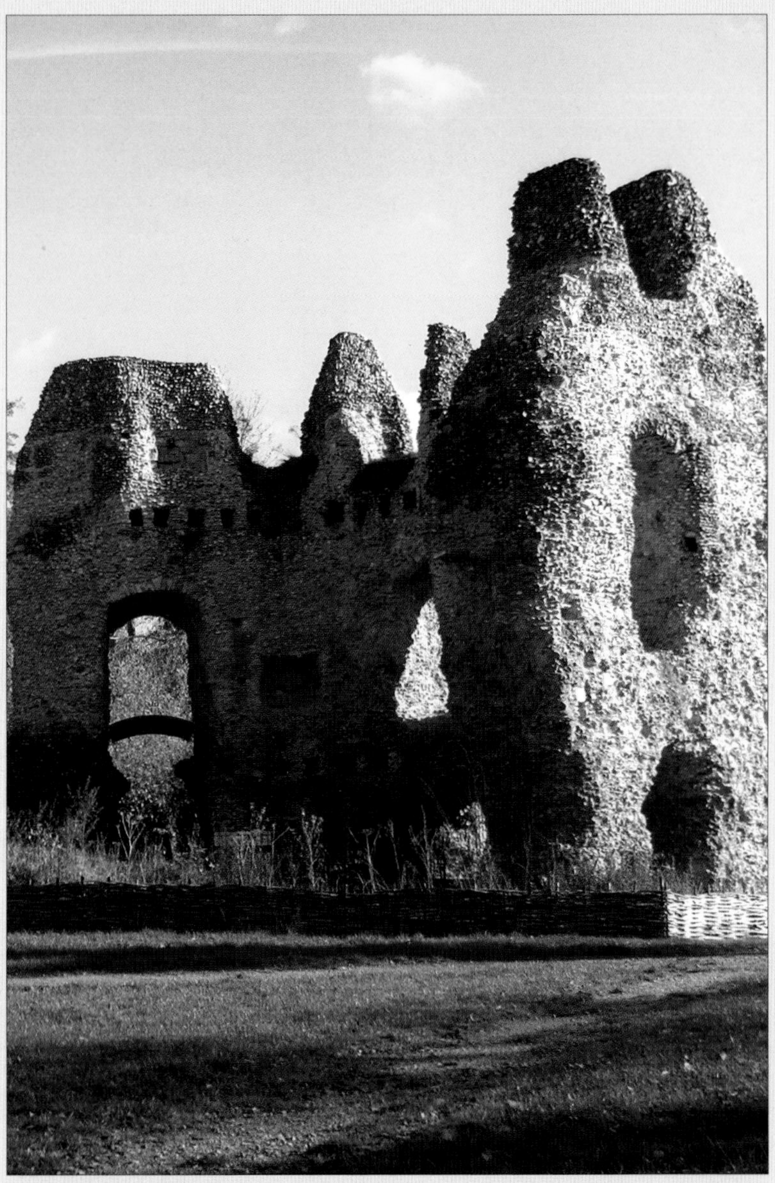

Odiham Castle

At the end of a brisk walk, it's time to consider the inner man and woman. You'll find plenty of places to stop for a cream tea or a meal in one of the Forest's welcoming pubs, and there are also opportunities to watch traditional cider making or buy some award-winning New Forest cheese.

On the other side of the county, the ink is scarcely dry on the rolling chalk hills of the South Downs National Park, to be launched in 2011. The high downland stretches from Winchester to Eastbourne but, within

Hampshire, the Park also includes the upper Itchen Valley and the gentler countryside north of Petersfield.

The history of this latest National Park is as diverse as its landscape. Walking through these pages you'll discover prehistoric fortifications and a Civil War battlefield, as well as the inn where Charles Kingsley wrote much of his children's fable *The Water Babies*. Farther east, sporting history was made on a windswept hill near Hambledon, and you can still sit and watch the cricket from the pub where the English summer game was nurtured more than 200 years ago.

South Downs history and wildlife come together in Selborne, home of the eminent 18th-century naturalist Reverend Gilbert White. Your walk explores the beech hangers on the slopes high above the village, before descending the zigzag path that the great man built within a stone's throw of his former home opposite the church. The area is renowned for its wild flowers, and over 35 species of butterfly have been recorded locally.

Much of the chalk downland that Gilbert White would have known is now under the plough. Nevertheless, butterflies like the chalk-hill blue, silver-spotted skipper, and the Duke of Burgundy still fly above the unimproved grassland that you'll see in places like Beacon Hill and Butser Hill. In spring and summer, the close-cropped turf is bright with wildflowers, including yellow rattle, rock rose and several species of orchid.

Time to explore

These walks will take you across the length and breadth of the county, discovering the best of Hampshire's countryside and National Parks. Along the way, you'll touch on long-distance routes like the Wayfarers' Walk, the Test Way, and the South Downs Way National Trail. Hampshire is well provided with more than a dozen of these recreational trails and, if you'd like to explore further, you'll find a selection on the County Council's website at www3.hants.gov.uk/longdistance.htm

But for now, it's time to start walking – so turn the page, and we'll set off ...

This book includes a list of waypoints alongside the description of the walk, so that you can enjoy the full benefits of gps should you wish to. For more information on using your gps, read the *Pathfinder® Guide GPS for Walkers,* by gps teacher and navigation trainer, Clive Thomas (ISBN 978-0-7117-4445-5). For essential information on map reading and basic navigation, read the *Pathfinder® Guide Map Reading Skills* by outdoor writer, Terry Marsh (ISBN 978-0-7117-4978-8). Both titles are available in bookshops or can be ordered online at www.totalwalking.co.uk

Bishop's Dyke, New Forest

Start	Pig Bush car park, on B3056 south-east of Beaulieu Road Station
Distance	$2\frac{1}{4}$ miles (3.8km)
Height gain	100 feet (30m)
Approximate time	1 hour
Parking	At the start
Route terrain	Heath and woodland paths that will be muddy in the wet
Dog friendly	Dogs must be led near grazing animals
Ordnance Survey maps	Landranger 196 (The Solent & Isle of Wight), Explorer OL22 (New Forest)

GPS waypoints

Start	SU 362 050
A	SU 363 047
B	SU 356 041
C	SU 351 043
D	SU 355 048
E	SU 357 052
F	SU 359 050

This walk allows you to enjoy a typical mixture of New Forest scenery within a surprisingly short distance. It goes across heath and through woodland, then crosses and recrosses Bishop's Dyke, a 13th-century bank and ditch which encircles an area of bog. Duckboards give easy access to the bog and allow a close view of some of the fascinating plants that inhabit this wetland. The gentle sloping heathland that follows is popular with the tiny bird, the Dartford warbler.

The ponies of the forest are owned by commoners with the right to 'Common of Pasture'. This right, which it is thought goes back to the time when William the Conqueror turned the forest into a hunting preserve, allows a commoner to graze his or her stock on the forest. This is usually ponies but can also be cattle, some donkeys and latterly a few sheep. Ponies are branded with the owner's individual brand so that they can be quickly recognised.

Delightful woodland at Rowbarrow

Leave through the wood on the opposite side of the car park to the road, taking a narrow path about halfway along this side. The path soon comes out of the wood on the opposite side. Turn left here and walk along the sandy path running around the woodland edge. Continue until you reach a T-junction where a gravel track crosses your route **A**.

Turn right, cross the footbridge over Shepton Water, and follow the track across the heath.

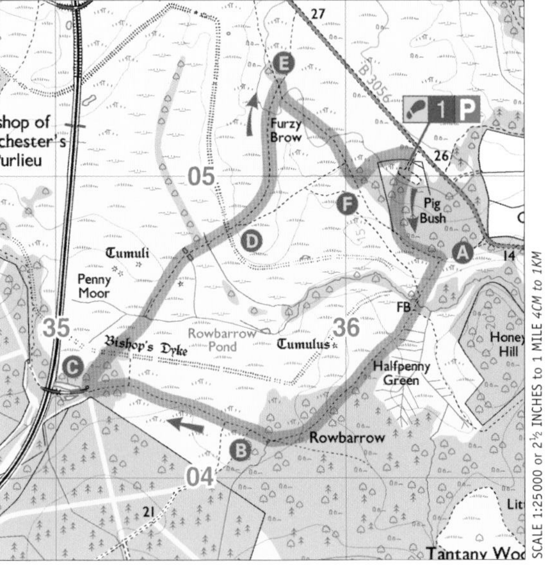

SCALE 1:25 000 or 2½ INCHES to 1 MILE *4CM to 1KM*

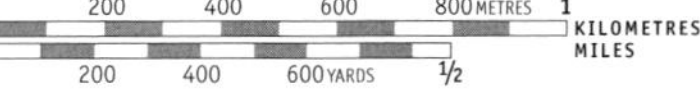

Over 14 different species of tree and shrub can be found to the left beside this stream. Also on the left is Halfpenny Green. There are a number of halfpenny greens in Hampshire, and the name is an apt description of their size. Beyond the heath your way continues into light woodland, a good area for spotting wrens, woodpeckers, tree creepers and nuthatches. Now less well-defined, the track dives into Rowbarrow woods, curves around to the right, and crosses a ditch before emerging from the woods **B**.

Continue along a wide grassy ride, fringed with bracken and heather to left and right. From here you can see the Bishop's Dyke out to your right. This ancient earthwork encompasses an area of about 500 acres, and it is thought that it was built around 1284. The then Bishop of Winchester, John de Pontoise, was offered an area of land that he could crawl around in a day. It is said that, wanting the largest area possible, he spent 24 hours on hands and knees.

The grass ride bears to the left to arrive at a bridge over the main Bournemouth to Southampton railway line. The small fenced enclosure here is a pony pound. Each autumn in the New Forest there are pony round-ups, known as 'The Drifts'. The ponies are herded into these pounds, found throughout the forest, where they are checked, branded and wormed. At this point a pony may be returned to the forest or sent on to the Pony Sales. These sales take place across the way from Beaulieu Road Station in an area of wooden railed pens that can be seen from the road.

Twenty yards short of the pony pound **C**, double back onto a grassy path fringed by bracken and silver birch trees. The path crosses the Bishop's Dyke and heads across the heath towards a sandy scar on the near horizon. This area will be quite boggy in wet weather. Continue over a wooden footbridge and a short shingle causeway, followed by a second, longer causeway before the sandy path begins to climb towards Furzy Brow. Cross Bishop's Dyke **D**, fork left, and continue towards a large rounded clump of trees. Just before reaching the trees, double back to your right **E** onto a slightly narrower sandy path. Pass a lone pine tree and continue to a crossways at the corner of the wood behind Pig Bush car park **F**. Turn left here and follow the woodland edge gently uphill for just over 200 yds; now turn right at the lone pine tree, back into the car park. ●

New Forest snapshot

Start	Millyford Bridge car park, one mile west of Emery Down on the back road to Linwood
Distance	2¾ miles (4.5km)
Height gain	130 feet (40m)
Approximate time	1½ hours
Parking	At the start
Route terrain	Forest tracks and paths that may be muddy in wet weather
Dog friendly	Dogs must be led near grazing animals
Ordnance Survey maps	Landranger 195 (Bournemouth & Purbeck), Explorer OL22 (New Forest)

GPS waypoints

- SU 267 079 (start)
- Ⓐ SU 264 078
- Ⓑ SU 270 070
- Ⓒ SU 269 064
- Ⓓ SU 263 064
- Ⓔ SU 264 070

This short walk visits three of the New Forest's best-known sites. From the car park it crosses a typical forest road, bordered by old and ornamental trees, to pass the Portuguese Fireplace. In the First World War this was part of the cookhouse of a Portuguese army camp with troops living in huts nearby. The walk then takes a woodland route to the New Forest Reptile Centre where examples of all the region's reptiles can be seen. Passing over a small heath, the route then visits the Knightwood Oak, one of the most ancient trees in the New Forest.

Leave Millyford Bridge car park by going back onto the road and turning right. Almost immediately, on the opposite side of the road there is a grassed area. Walk to the right of it to visit the Portuguese Fireplace. During the First World War, Portuguese troops were stationed in the New Forest to help produce vitally important timber. There was a great shortage of local manpower at the time as most forest workers were doing military service. To ensure that meals were cooked in the traditional way, troops constructed this fireplace. It now stands as a memorial to their assistance.

Continue ahead along the side of the road for 170 yds until a five-bar gate can be seen on the left Ⓐ. Turn left and go through the gate into the inclosure.

Follow the gravel track ahead. After 150 yds the track divides; fork left and follow the main track, ignoring all turnings until you reach the Reptile Centre car park.

Large open-air enclosures hold all the native reptiles and amphibians found in the New Forest: grass snake, adder, slow worm, smooth snake plus sand and common lizard, newt, common toad and frog. All reptile numbers have declined in Britain, due mainly to loss of habitat. Smooth snake and sand lizard are now found almost nowhere else in Britain except Dorset and the

New Forest. Apart from providing an opportunity for visitors to view some of these fascinating and shy creatures, the Reptile Centre breeds rarer reptiles for release back into the forest.

After your visit, leave the Centre through the gate beside the cattle-grid, with the keeper's cottage on your left.

Turn right onto the grassy path opposite the cottage **B** and pass a lone pine tree. Now follow the path as it winds through the heather and then widens out to follow the right-hand side of Warwick Slade Heath. Continue along the path which heads for the fence and road beyond. Just before reaching the fence bear right over a footbridge **C**.

Follow the path through the bracken, bear to your right away from the road, and cross the clearing to reach a gate into Knightwood Inclosure. Follow the forest ride through the trees and bear right to reach the Knightwood Oak surrounded by its protective fence.

This pollarded oak tree is estimated to be at least 400 years old. At the time when it was young most trees in the New Forest were cut back to produce numbers of young branches probably used for fuel and charcoal. This resulted in hugh trunks and short trees that took up a large expanse of ground space, so in 1698 William III brought in an act forbidding pollarding. This helps in determining the age of trees as most old pollarded oaks and beech in the New Forest are likely to have been planted before this act came into force.

From the Knightwood Oak, continue along the gravel path to see the young oak trees presented by the Queen, the Duke of Edinburgh and others to commemorate recent events and landmark dates. Bear right, and follow the gravel path to a road opposite the Knightwood Oak car park.

Turn right along the road and then, almost immediately, branch off to the right **D** onto a path leading into the woods.

Follow this wide path bordered by old wellingtonias, giant conifers easily recognised by their cork-like bark. The path crosses a clearing, then climbs gently to meet a gravel track at a bend **E**.

Bear right onto the track, go through a gate, and keep ahead for just over ½ mile until it leaves the inclosure through the gate where you originally entered it. Then walk along beside the road back into the car park on the left. ●

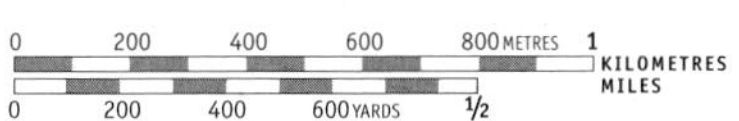

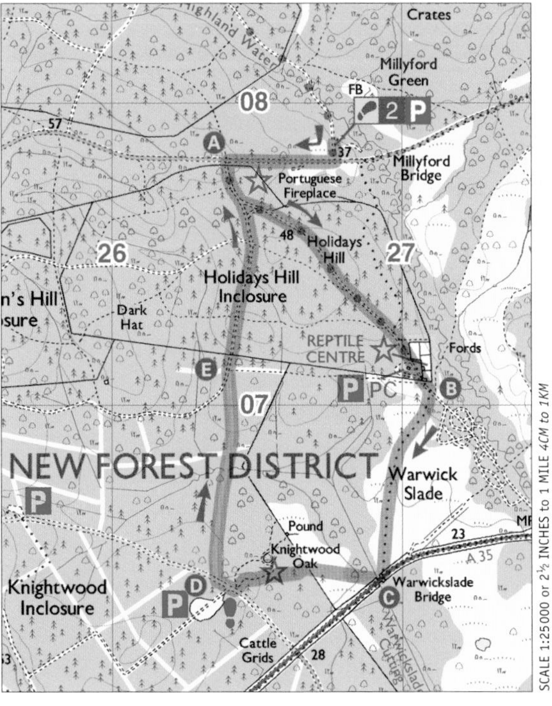

SCALE 1:25000 or 2½ INCHES to 1 MILE *4CM to 1KM*

Winchester's water meadows

		GPS waypoints
Start	Tun Bridge car park, Garnier Road	[start] SU 483 280
Distance	3 miles (5km)	Ⓐ SU 479 268
Height gain	n/a	Ⓑ SU 475 271
Approximate time	1½ hours	Ⓒ SU 479 282
Parking	At the start	Ⓓ SU 485 287
Route terrain	Gravel and field edge paths that will be muddy in the wet	
Dog friendly	Dogs must be led near grazing animals	
Ordnance Survey maps	Landranger 185 (Winchester & Basingstoke), Explorer 132 (Winchester)	

After following the old Twyford road south between the Itchen Navigation and a former railway line, the route turns sharply to avoid the motorway. Now it leads through tranquil water meadows to the Hospital of St Cross. Beyond St Cross, the walk passes close to Winchester College and the former Bishop's palace at Wolvesey, as well as the Cathedral and city centre.

Described by Simon Jenkins as 'England's oldest and most perfect almshouse', the Hospital of St Cross was founded in the early 1130s by Henry de Blois. Henry was a grandson of William the Conqueror and, at that time, Bishop of Winchester. Originally built for 'thirteen men, feeble and so reduced in strength that they can scarcely ... support themselves without other aid', the Hospital also provided a daily meal for 100 other deserving poor persons. The Brethren's Hall, Georgian kitchen, Tudor ambulatory and flower gardens are all open to visitors, together with a gift shop and summer **tearoom**.

Almost half the walk follows the Itchen Navigation, built in the 17th century to carry coals from Southampton to Winchester.

Face the Navigation and turn left, walking between the bollards to follow the well-made waterside path that squeezes between the old railway embankment and the canal on your right. Just past the wooden gates leading into Plague Pits Valley and St Catherine's Hill nature reserve, look out for the remains of an old canal lock half-hidden in the trees on your right. Soon the path sweeps left and right under the old railway, and a roar of traffic heralds your approach to the nearby motorway.

Turn right along the former Five Bridges Road Ⓐ, following the quiet pedestrian route towards St Cross, Stanmore and Winchester. Re-cross the old railway at a broken bridge, go through a gate, and continue across the main river bridge until you reach a metal traffic barrier and a turning on your right B.

Turn right here, following the waymarked footpath over a couple of stiles into a field. Walk along the left-hand field edge beside the stream to a further stile at the approach to St Cross Hospital. Nip across, and continue with the stream on your left through a short avenue of trees to a kissing-gate at the corner of the graveyard. Keep ahead beside the railings to the corner of the Hospital wall, then bear right as the signposted footpath heads across the grass to a footbridge and kissing-gate. Still with the stream on your left, continue past red brick houses to the junction with Garnier Road C.

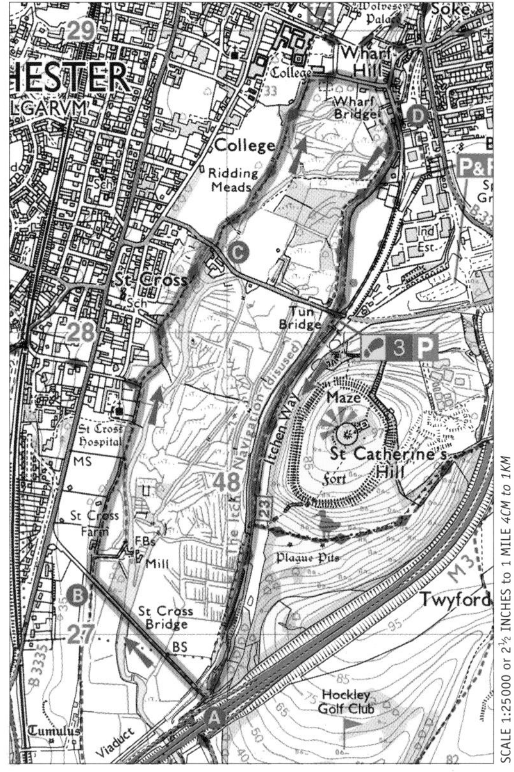

SCALE 1:25000 or 2½ INCHES to 1 MILE *4CM to 1KM*

0 200 400 600 800 METRES 1 KILOMETRES
0 200 400 600 YARDS ½ MILES

Zigzag right and left across the river bridge, following the riverside path past a footbridge to the College playing fields across the water on your left. Continue along the riverbank towards the green copper roof of New Hall, then turn right along the College access road to the junction with College Walk. You can turn left here for a short diversion to visit Wolvesey Castle, the Cathedral, College and city centre. Keep ahead to continue the walk, crossing the Navigation at Blackbridge House before Wharf Hill swings off to your left. Turn right here, pass Wharf House, and follow the private road for 130 yds.

St Cross Hospital

Now dive off down the narrow Pilgrim's Trail beside the gate to number 2, New Barge Cottages D. Turn left, and walk beside the water all the way back to meet Garnier Road at Tun Bridge car park where your walk began. ●

Ashmansworth and Crux Easton

Start	Ashmansworth war memorial, on the village green
Distance	3 miles (5km)
Height gain	280 feet (85m)
Approximate time	1½ hours
Parking	Roadside parking near the village centre
Route terrain	Country lanes, tracks and field paths, which will be muddy in the wet
Dog friendly	Please lead dogs along the on-road sections
Ordnance Survey maps	Landranger 174 (Newbury & Wantage), Explorer 144 (Basingstoke)

GPS waypoints

- SU 415 574
- Ⓐ SU 420 580
- Ⓑ SU 430 575
- Ⓒ SU 426 564
- Ⓓ SU 421 567
- Ⓔ SU 414 570

The walk begins on the green in Hampshire's highest village, a straggling rural community of brick and flint houses. There are stunning views into Berkshire as you follow the Wayfarer's Walk along the ridge some 760 feet (233m) above sea level, before turning south to the fascinating little hamlet of Crux Easton.

A Warminster man, John Wallis Titt, built the Simplex wind engine at Crux Easton in about 1891. The engine ground corn and pumped water from the adjacent well, and is thought to be the only one of its kind in southern England still standing on its original site. The well house contains a small museum, and is open on some summer Sundays – see www.hampshiremills.org for opening times.

Head north east along the village road towards Newbury, keeping straight on past the telephone box at the turning for East Woodhay.

Turn right at the crossways Ⓐ along the signposted byway that forms part of the long-distance Wayfarer's Walk from Inkpen Beacon to Emsworth. There are far-reaching views along this section and, a little farther on, look out for the imposing bulk of Highclere Castle about a mile across the valley to your left. A stately home in all but name, the castle stands on the site of a medieval palace once owned by the Bishops of Winchester. Sir Charles Barry, fresh from his leading role in rebuilding the Houses of Parliament, extensively remodelled the building in the mid-19th century. Highclere is now the home of the Earl and Countess of Carnarvon, whose family has lived here since 1679.

Cross the busy A343 with care at Three Legged Cross, walking in front of the former pub before turning right along the lane towards Crux Easton Ⓑ. Continue until the lane bears left just past Field House, then fork right through a metal field gate onto the

Crux Easton – wind engine

signposted footpath. Bear half-right across the open field to a stile in the hedge, then head just to the right of the wind engine at Crux Easton as you continue across a second field to a stile beside a wooden gate.

It's worth spending the time to explore Crux Easton. The wind engine stands just across the road from here, and the little Georgian church is a couple of hundred yards farther on down the lane. Turn right down the signposted byway **C** to continue the walk, and follow the lane around the double bends. Just beyond the brick cottages on your right the byway bends to the left; keep ahead here down the signposted footpath that leads you across a field to the A343 **D**.

Take care once again as you cross this road, then nip over the stile and walk up the hill to the double stile straight ahead. Continue over the brow and down to a stile in the left-hand corner of the woods ahead. Now follow the left-hand woodland edge up the hill to cross another stile before bearing right and following the right-hand edge of the next two fields. Cross the stile at the top corner of the second field to join the enclosed path that ends at a final stile opposite Steeles Farm **E**.

You can turn left here to visit the church, which stands just off the lane to your right close to Church Farm and the former home of the composer Gerald Finzi. Turn right to complete the walk, and follow the village road back to the war memorial. ●

0 200 400 600 800 METRES 1 KILOMETRES
0 200 400 600 YARDS ½ MILES

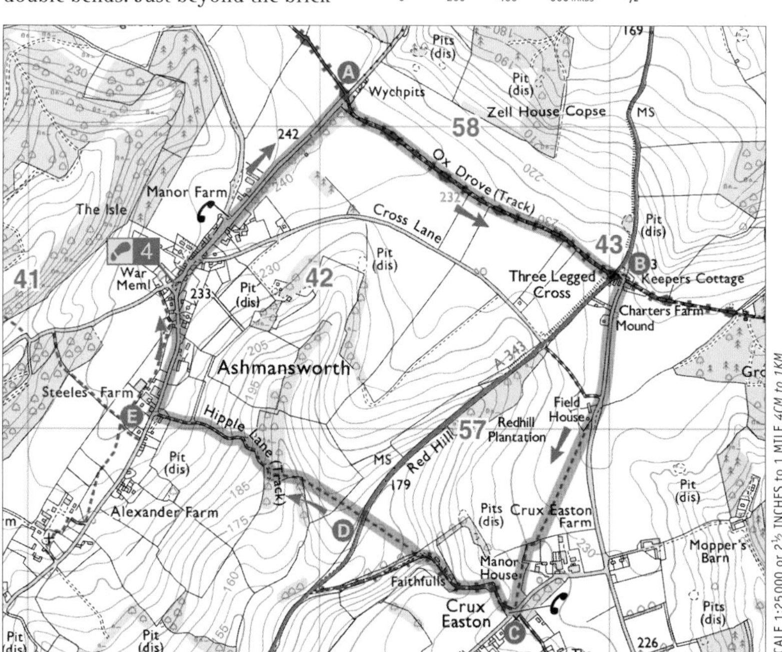

The Itchen Valley

Start	Car park near the lake on the lane from Easton to Avington
Distance	3½ miles (5.5km)
Height gain	180 feet (55m)
Approximate time	1½ hours
Parking	At the start
Route terrain	Country lanes and field paths that will be muddy in the wet
Dog friendly	Dogs must be led on roads and near grazing animals
Ordnance Survey maps	Landranger 185 (Winchester & Basingstoke), Explorer 132 (Winchester)

GPS waypoints

Start	SU 528 320
A	SU 515 322
B	SU 515 327
C	SU 534 328
D	SU 530 319

The River Itchen is one of Hampshire's most famous chalk streams and the valley's wildlife, meadows and flood pastures are nationally important. This short, easy walk explores one of the prettiest sections, crossing the river in two places and passing through the delightful village of Avington. The area is home to rare insects like the southern damselfly, while trout, salmon and crayfish live in the river itself. It's a good place for birdwatching too, and much of the valley between Cheriton and Kings Worthy is officially designated as a Site of Special Scientific Interest.

Avington received its charter from King Edgar, and King Henry VIII later granted the estate to Edmund Clerke, who built the original banqueting hall. George Brydges improved and enlarged Clerke's house in the mid-17th century to entertain King Charles II and Nell Gwynne, and Brydges' cousin, the third Duke of Chandos, later laid out the grounds. Avington Park is still a private house and the house and gardens are open in the summer months. There are full details of the opening times at www.avingtonpark.co.uk

On the edge of Avington Park, the walk passes a rare time capsule – the unrestored Georgian church of St Mary. Completed in 1771, the red brick building is dominated by its crenellated tower and approached along a pathway of old tombstones. Inside, the high box pews are made of Spanish mahogany thought to have come from a captured Armada galleon.

(Start) Turn right out of the car park and follow the wide roadside verge past Avington Lake, where there are good views of the house behind you. Cross the cattle-grid, crest the low summit, and drop down the hill past Easton Lodge. Continue for 200 yds past the village name sign, as far as the White House on your right (A).

Turn right up the signposted footpath

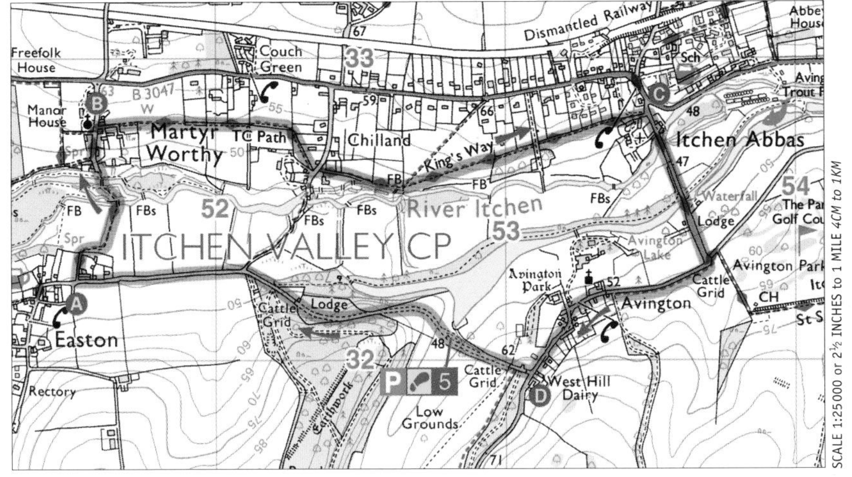

SCALE 1:25 000 or 2½ INCHES to 1 MILE *4CM to 1KM*

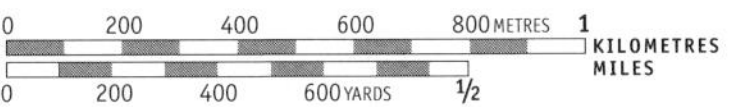

that follows the gravelled drive towards Paidon. Go through the small metal gate at the end of the drive and follow the winding path beside the wire fence on your left to the footbridges over the River Itchen. Cross over, and keep ahead up the lane into Martyr Worthy as far as St Swithun's church **B**.

Turn right along the signposted footpath opposite the church, continue through a kissing-gate, and keep ahead along the grassy path across the fields. Pass a metal field gate on your left, and carry on through two more kissing-gates; the path bears right after a third kissing-gate, and continues between fences to reach the lane at Chilland.

Door of Easton church

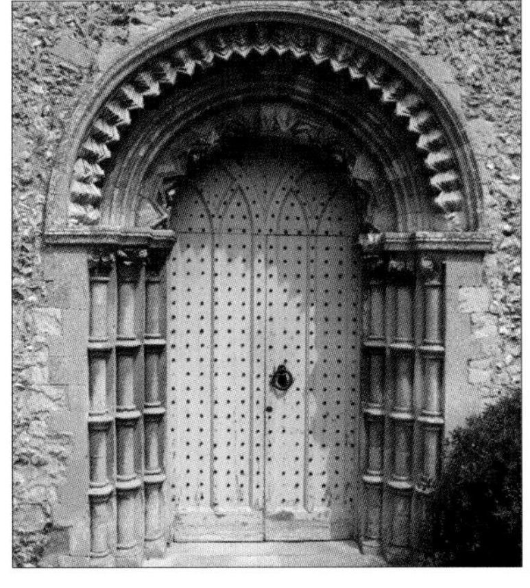

Turn left, then almost immediately right along the enclosed path that meets the river at another kissing-gate. Bear just slightly left here, following the wooden fence on your left and bearing gently away from the river on your right. Two more kissing-gates lead you across a gravelled drive, and the path continues between fences to the lane **C** at Itchen Abbas church. Turn left, then right here, for the few paces to **The Trout Inn**.

Turn right and follow the lane over several bridges and past the entrance gates to Avington Park. Keep left at the road junction; then, almost at once, double back through a former kissing-gate at the golf course entrance to join the path that runs parallel with the road on your right. Rejoin the road at a kissing-gate and continue past St Mary's church, following the road as it winds through Avington village to a road junction **D** 200 yds beyond the well head.

Turn right towards Easton and Winchester, then walk down the hill and over the cattle-grid to return to the start of your walk.

Holmsley's old railway and Whitten Pond

Start	Holmsley, New Forest; west of A35 and south of Burley
Distance	4 miles (6.5km). Shorter version $2\frac{3}{4}$ miles (4.5km)
Height gain	115 feet (35m) for both versions
Approximate time	2 hours ($1\frac{1}{2}$ hours for shorter route)
Parking	Forestry Commission Holmsley car park
Route terrain	Old railway path, heath and woodland tracks. The route is often muddy around Whitten Pond
Dog friendly	Dogs must be led near grazing animals
Ordnance Survey maps	Landranger 195 (Bournemouth & Purbeck), Explorer OL22 (New Forest)

GPS waypoints

- SU 222 011
- Ⓐ SU 216 011
- Ⓑ SU 203 012
- Ⓒ SU 204 016
- Ⓓ SU 221 014
- Ⓔ SU 231 006
- Ⓕ SU 228 009

This walk begins on Holmsley Ridge, an area of high heathland with views over the local New Forest. The path then drops down to Whitten Bottom and sparkling Whitten Pond before returning along the route of a disused railway line to visit the old station building – now a popular tearoom. A shorter route omits the visit to the old station and returns to the car park from point Ⓓ. Waterproof footwear is recommended after a spell of wet weather.

Holmsley Station was the first stop after leaving Brockenhurst on the original Southampton and Dorchester Railway. Holmsley served the nearby RAF airfield during the Second World War and the last train ran in 1964 – but you can still see an overgrown section of the original platform just before reaching the **Old Station Tea House**.

Leave the car park by the entrance and turn left onto the road. After 50 yds turn right onto a gravel track; pass the car barrier, and continue for 500 yds until the track bears to the left Ⓐ.

Fork right here onto a narrower grassy track, passing the shallow, disused gravel pit that lies behind the wire fence on your left. When the track divides, ignore the left-hand fork and continue straight ahead, following the path downhill towards two ponds. Head for the left-hand side of the larger pond; a stream flows into the pond here, and you'll need to make a small detour until you can step across easily. Now bear right around the water's edge until you reach the Whitten Pond signboard Ⓑ.

From here, take the sandy path that runs parallel with the road towards the trees on your right. Fork right about 100 yds before the trees, then continue across a shallow bank and down onto

The dismantled Brockenhurst – Ringwood railway line

the old railway line C.

Turn right and follow the old line through a heather-clad cutting and out onto the low embankment, with good views over the boggy heath. After about 1¼ miles you'll come to a striking modern house on the site of the old level crossing keeper's cottage at Holmsley Passage D.

You can cut the walk short by turning right at this point and following the lane back to the car park.

To complete the full route, cross the lane and continue along the old railway. The trail becomes more shaded as it runs through an avenue of young oak trees and crosses the two bridges that herald the approach to Holmsley Station. Just after the second bridge, look out for the old platform in the undergrowth on your right. At the end of the trail, go through the gate in the fence; the entrance to the **Old Station Tea House** E is just across the road to your right.

Return from the Tea House following your outward route past the old platform and across the two bridges.

Immediately after the second bridge F, turn left onto a path that runs down the side of the low embankment and across a small sleeper footbridge. Now follow the well-made path through the wooded bog for about 200 yds until you reach the five-bar gate leading into Holmsley Inclosure. Keep ahead through the gate to a complex junction 50 yds farther on. Ignore the turnings left and right, and follow the main track that curves gently right, climbing gradually between areas of coniferous and deciduous woodland. The track leaves the woods through a gate opposite Holmsley Lodge; turn right here, cross the cattle-grid, and walk beside the road for the short distance back to the car park. ●

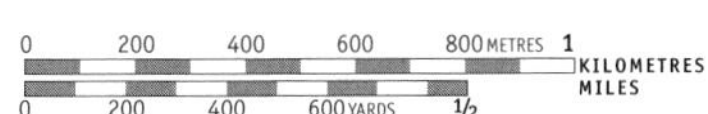

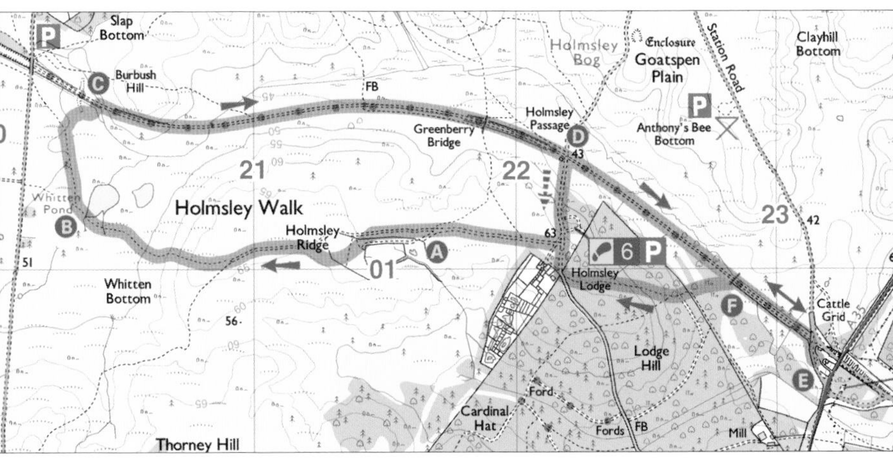

Warsash waterside and woodland

Start	Passage Lane car park, Warsash
Distance	4 miles (6.3km)
Height gain	130 feet (40m)
Approximate time	2 hours
Parking	At the start
Route terrain	Mainly well-made coastal and woodland paths
Dog friendly	Please lead dogs and scoop the poop in the woodland park and nature reserve
Ordnance Survey maps	Landranger 196 (The Solent & Isle of Wight), Explorer 119 (Meon Valley, Portsmouth, Gosport & Fareham)

GPS waypoints

Start	SU 489 062
A	SU 489 075
B	SU 489 084
C	SU 497 081
D	SU 497 078

This is a walk in two halves. Setting off from Warsash, the route follows the Solent Way along a narrow causeway between the lower reaches of the River Hamble and a series of tidal lagoons. Turning inland, the walk threads its way past the lakes and waterfalls of Holly Hill Woodland Park, before cutting back through a local nature reserve to rejoin the Solent Way.

After the wide-open vistas of the Hamble with its seabirds, sailing yachts and characteristic moorings, the walk climbs gently up Crableck Lane to reach the woodland park. It was laid out in the 1880s by Quintin Hogg – grandfather of the eponymous Conservative politician. George Winn, who built the privately owned Edwardian mansion near the main entrance to the park, later bought Holly Hill.

Do make time at the end of your walk to take the short ferry trip across the river to explore the village of Hamble-le-Rice; details of the service are posted at www.hamble-warsashferry.co.uk

Wrecked hull at Warsash

Leave the car park by the gap next to the public toilets and turn right onto the Solent Way footpath. Pass the pink Hamble Ferry shelter and follow the winding causeway beside the River Hamble with

its wide views to Hamble-le-Rice on the western shore.

Keep ahead beside the river when a path turns off to your right beside a seat that was donated by Locks Heath Rotary Club. Cross a footbridge spanning the entrance to the lagoon on your right and pass a footpath that turns off across the long wooden footbridge on your right Ⓐ.

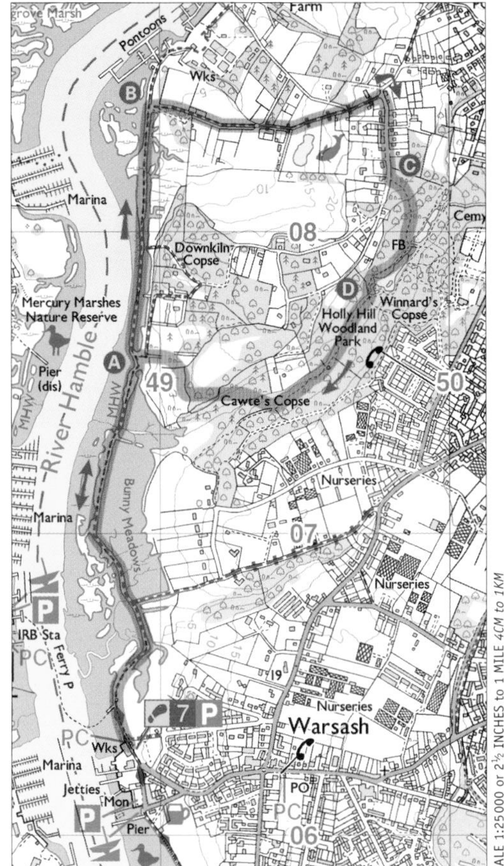

0 200 400 600 800 METRES 1 KILOMETRES
0 200 400 600 YARDS ½ MILES

At the end of the lagoon the path opens out as you approach an area of dense moorings ahead. Turn right here up the narrow, tree-shaded footpath Ⓑ that runs parallel with a wider track just to your right. The path merges with the track at a wooden signpost where you keep ahead along the byway, continuing onto Crableck Lane to a T-junction with Holly Hill Lane. Cross over and turn right along the pavement for 300 yds.

Turn left through a metal gate into Holly Hill Woodland Park Ⓒ. Keep ahead past two metal barriers, following the green waymarked route that curves gently down through Winnard's Copse to a crossways with a footbridge ahead. Turn right here, walking beside the ponds and waterfalls on your left to cross a footbridge at the foot of the slope Ⓓ.

Turn right here towards Hamble Foreshore, following the winding woodland path with a stream on your right. Cross a wooden causeway and keep ahead down the valley, then cross a wooden footbridge and turn right at the next junction, still signposted towards Hamble Foreshore. Join a boardwalk, then fork right down the hill and over a footbridge into Hook with Warsash Nature Reserve.

Follow the winding woodland path up a set of steps and out into a clearing overlooking the river. Turn right onto the grassy path along the top of the clearing, then re-enter the woods and bear left at a junction with another path that drops gently down towards the river. Go through a gap beside a wooden gate to rejoin the Solent Way at point Ⓐ.

Turn left here, and retrace your outward route beside the river to the car park. ●

Silchester's Roman town

Start	English Heritage Roman Town Trail car park
Distance	4 miles (6.5km)
Height gain	280 feet (85m)
Approximate time	2 hours
Parking	At the start
Route terrain	Mostly rural tracks and paths, with some muddy sections in the wet
Dog friendly	Dogs must be led near farm animals
Ordnance Survey maps	Landranger 175 (Reading & Windsor), Explorer 159 (Reading)

GPS waypoints

- SU 635 629
- Ⓐ SU 633 634
- Ⓑ SU 643 643
- Ⓒ SU 648 641
- Ⓓ SU 644 625
- Ⓔ SU 636 625

The Roman town of Calleva Atrebatum is one of Hampshire's eternal mysteries. It was abandoned in the 6th or 7th century and now lies sleeping beneath the Hampshire farmland. This walk explores the wooded countryside to the north of the old town before finishing with Calleva's two great glories – its Roman amphitheatre and massive outer walls.

The Romans developed the established Iron Age settlement at Silchester into a fortified administrative capital and trading centre covering some 79 acres. At the heart of its distinctive street pattern lay the forum basilica, surrounded by shops, inns and work-shops. You can see a large display of exhibits found at the site in the Silchester Collection at Reading Museum.

Leave the car park through the metal height barrier, cross the road and keep ahead up the signposted gravel byway. Ignore all turnings and continue until the byway meets a road.

Turn right for 25 yds, then right again onto another signposted byway Ⓐ. (Keep ahead up the road for a short diversion to **The Red Lion inn.**) The tarmac byway climbs past Lovegroves Cottage, then levels off to reach a crossways at Lovegrove Farm. Keep ahead through a metal farm gate, pass the buildings of West End Farm on your right, and continue downhill towards a large electricity pylon.

Here the track bends left; follow it for 100 yds, then turn left beside the woods and continue uphill through a metal gate to follow the woodland edge on your right. Continue through a gate at the top corner of the woods and keep ahead across the open field towards a cluster of brick houses where the path meets a road Ⓑ.

Cross over and turn right along the pavement to pass **The Turner's Arms.** Continue for 125 yds, then cross back and turn right over a wooden footbridge to join a signposted footpath. Follow the right-hand field edge to begin with, then go through the gap at the waymark post and continue between fences to reach a road. Turn right and walk 100 yds

Roman walls and church

to a fork at Longview Ⓒ.

Fork right along the no through road and keep ahead at a bridleway signpost, where a footpath turns off to the right. Pass the buildings at Simms Stud Farm and keep ahead along a narrower sunken track. Cross the stream at the foot of the hill and bear left across a narrow field into Nine Acre Copse. Follow the path through the woods until you reach the woodland edge at a former stile.

Now keep ahead across an open field, cross the stile, and continue beneath the power lines across the next field. The path drops to cross a stile and footbridge, then climbs again and bears right to follow the left-hand field edge. Bear left, then right, through a gap at the top corner of the field to join a rough farm track. Pass the entrance to The Mount on your right and keep ahead briefly until you meet a road by a letterbox Ⓓ – the entrance to the 4,500-seat Roman amphitheatre is just here on your right.

Keep ahead past the turning on your left and continue along the lane past the 12th-century Church of St Mary the Virgin. Keep the Roman walls on your right, and branch off the road to your right at a gate. Now simply follow the walls all the way into a wooded area, and continue until the path meets a junction with the gravel track that bisects the Roman town Ⓔ.

Turn sharp left here and follow the Roman Town Trail as it zigzags right and left through a gate, then back along an enclosed path to the start of the walk. ●

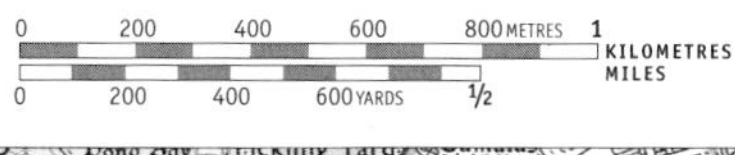

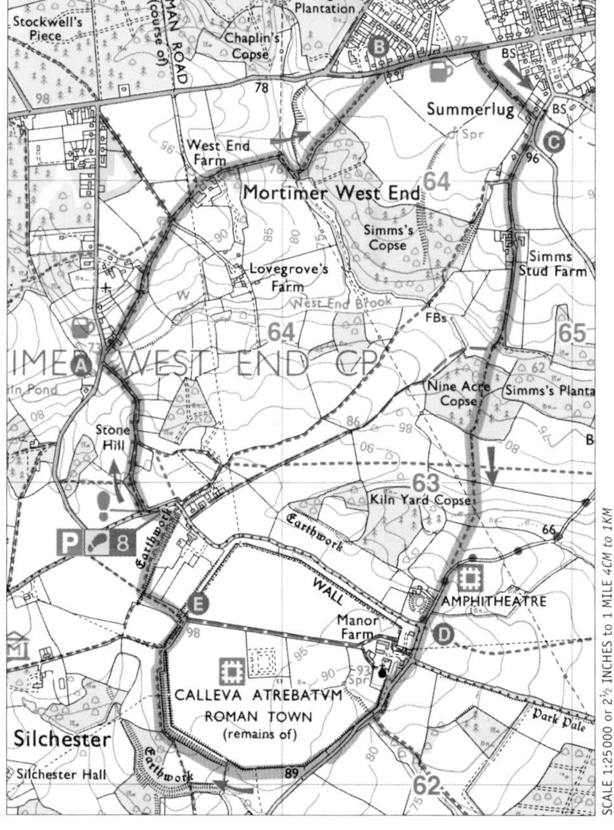

Odiham and the Basingstoke Canal

Start	Odiham Wharf car park, London Road, Odiham
Distance	4½ miles (7.3km)
Height gain	150 feet (45m)
Approximate time	2 hours
Parking	At the start
Route terrain	Town streets, rural paths and canal towpath
Dog friendly	Dogs must be led through Greywell moors nature reserve and near grazing animals
Ordnance Survey maps	Landranger 186 (Aldershot & Guildford), Explorer 144 (Basingstoke, Alton & Whitchurch)

GPS waypoints

- Start: SU 747 516
- A: SU 732 508
- B: SU 718 510
- C: SU 732 517

Setting off through the appealing little market town of Odiham, the walk strikes out across farmland to Greywell village before concluding with a delightful waterside stroll along the Basingstoke Canal towpath. It's worth taking the time to explore Odiham, and there's also plenty to look at along the way. The route winds through Greywell Moors nature reserve, crosses a disused canal tunnel and passes the ruins of Odiham Castle.

Walk back up London Road past the **Waterwitch** pub and bear right along the High Street. Cross the road opposite the **George Hotel** and walk up the narrow alley straight in front of you. Bear right at the top of the alley into The Bury, then turn left into All Saints churchyard.

Now turn immediately right along the wide gravelled path that leaves the churchyard between high walls. Cross Alton Road by **The Crown restaurant and bar** and continue along the enclosed path and beside playing fields to reach Recreation Road. Turn right, then left into West Street and walk past Robert May's school.

Just beyond the school, turn right up the steps **A** onto a signposted footpath; then, after 80 yds, turn left over the stile and strike half-right across the open

field to the stile on the far side. Cross the road, go through the gap in the opposite hedge, and bear right across the corner of the field. Go through the next hedge gap, heading diagonally to the gap in the left-hand corner of the next field, then turn right beside a steel barrier to reach Bidden Road.

Cross the road, turn left along the verge for 50 yds and turn right through a gap in the hedge. Now bear left and follow the path across the field, heading gently downhill to a kissing-gate hidden in the hedge at the entrance to Greywell Moors nature reserve. Keep ahead past the E C Wallace memorial stone to a second kissing-gate; cross the river and a squeeze-stile, then bear left and walk parallel with the field edge on your left to reach the kissing-gate at St Mary's Church Ⓑ.

Turn right down the church path towards the village, then right again at the lychgate to follow the village road as far as the junction with Deptford Lane, just beyond the **Fox and Goose** pub. Turn right here, then almost immediately left up the waymarked footpath that leads up and over the eastern portal of Greywell tunnel. Follow the path as it swings to the right and drops down onto the towpath, then settle into your stride for the delightful waterside walk all the way back to Odiham Wharf.

After 1/4 mile, look out for Odiham Castle on your left. Built about 1207, this small fortress was constructed as a resting place where King John could stop and hunt on journeys from Windsor to Winchester. In 1216 the castle was beseiged for 15 days by the French, who were so impressed by the defenders' courage, that they were freed after they had surrendered.

Continue beneath Swan Bridge Ⓒ, named after the adjoining **Swan** pub, for the final 1 1/4 miles to the finish. The canal bends left, then right, before heading straight for Odiham with the A287 for company across the fields on your left. The long straight ends at Odiham Wharf, just beyond the London Road bridge; turn left here to return to the car park where your walk began. ●

0 200 400 600 800 METRES 1 KILOMETRES
MILES
0 200 400 600 YARDS 1/2

SCALE 1:25 000 or 2½ INCHES to 1 MILE *4CM to 1KM*

Cheriton & Hinton Ampner

Start	Cheriton war memorial, on the village green
Distance	4½ miles (7.4km)
Height gain	345 feet (105m)
Approximate time	2 hours
Parking	On-street parking along the back lane near the school
Route terrain	Bridleways, tracks and field edge paths, which will be muddy when wet
Dog friendly	Dogs should be led along the short lengths of public road
Ordnance Survey maps	Landranger 185 (Winchester & Basingstoke), Explorer 132 (Winchester)

GPS waypoints

Start	SU 582 284
A	SU 590 286
B	SU 595 283
C	SU 605 276
D	SU 589 272

Starting in the heart of Cheriton, the early stages of the walk pass the important Civil War battlefields just outside the village. The route continues along the boundary of Hinton Ampner park, where there are some excellent views of Ralph Dutton's grand neo-Georgian house.

Dutton's family had lived on the estate since 1597, but the original Tudor house was replaced in 1793 and enlarged in the mid-19th century. After inheriting the estate in 1935, Ralph Dutton began major improvements to the park and gardens, as well as a radical remodelling of the house that was finally completed in 1950. Sadly, much of the building was destroyed by fire just ten years later – but, undaunted, Dutton immediately began to rebuild. He died a bachelor in 1985 and left his estate to the National Trust.

Face the war memorial and fork right over the bridge along the back lane past the post office. Take the first turning right, cross the stream, and turn right past the school to the gate of Cheriton House. Now turn left, following the Wayfarer's Walk up a narrow enclosed path. Keep ahead along the right-hand hedge when the path opens out near the top of the hill, and jump the stile in the corner of the field.

Turn right, and follow the field edge as it bends around to the left. From here there's a good view across the valley to the battlefields on the rising ground towards Cheriton Wood. A stile at the corner of the field brings you to a crossways **A**.

Keep ahead to a second crossways for more views of the battlefields to your left. Turn right here, following the waymarked Wayfarer's Walk under a metal barrier and over a low hill to a further crossways and barrier **B**.

Leave the Wayfarer's Walk and turn left along Cheriton Lane, bearing right at a metal gate where the path continues between hedges. Just beyond

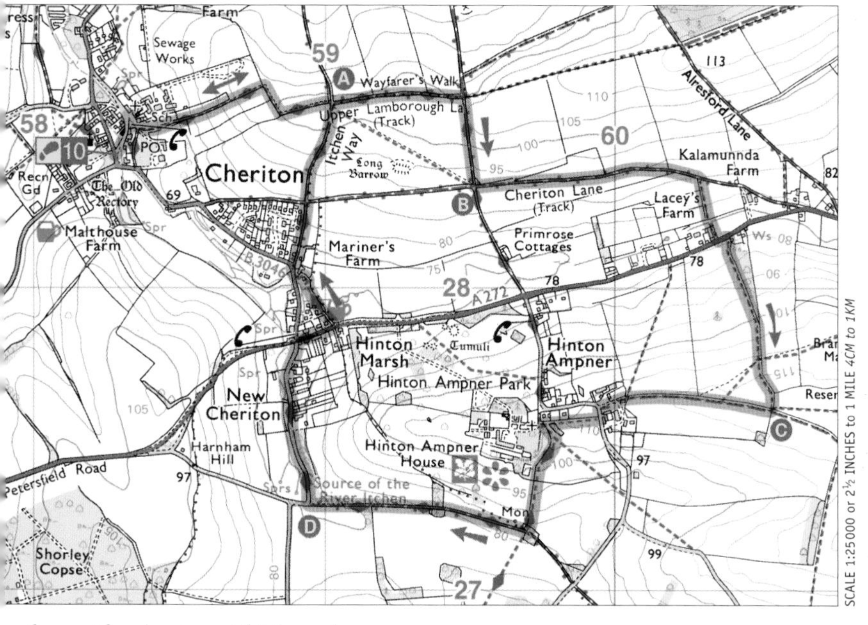

SCALE 1:25 000 or 2½ INCHES to 1 MILE 4CM to 1KM

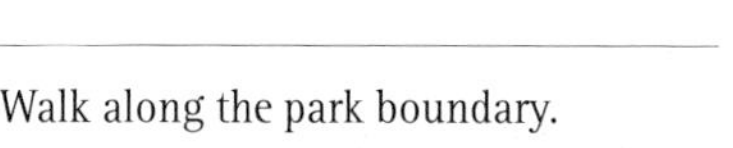

the next barrier, turn right through a gap by a metal gate and follow the hedge down to a yellow waymark on the corner of a garden fence. Turn left, then follow the fence around to the right to reach a stile at the A272.

Cross the road with care, turning left and then right onto the signposted footpath that climbs gently along the edge of an open field. Pass a stile in the hedge as the path levels off, and continue to a gap at the top corner of the field **C**.

Go through the gap and turn immediately right onto an attractive green bridleway that continues past a pair of brick cottages to meet a road at a bend. Turn left briefly, then right through a kissing-gate, and walk beside the wire fence to a pair of kissing-gates opposite All Saints Church.

Go through the first kissing-gate and turn left, rejoining the Wayfarer's Walk along an enclosed path that skirts the grounds of Hinton Ampner park and drops down into the valley. Go through a gate, then turn right along the valley bottom, still following the Wayfarer's Walk along the park boundary. Continue until the path meets Kilmeston Road at a bend **D**.

Turn right and follow the road through New Cheriton to the busy A272. Cross over and turn right along the pavement, then turn left opposite the **Hinton Arms** to follow the signposted footpath over a stile and along the left-hand field edge. Cross a plank bridge and then, as you approach the corner of the field, turn left over a stile and along the narrow path leading to the B3046. Turn right here onto the restricted byway, continuing past the houses and up a narrow sunken way to a crossways. Keep ahead as far as the next crossways, which you passed earlier **A**.

Turn left over the stile and walk along the left-hand field edge. Veer right at the corner of the field, then turn left over the stile and retrace your steps down the enclosed path into Cheriton village. ●

Selborne and Noar Hill

Start	Selborne
Distance	4¼ miles (7km)
Height gain	590 feet (180m)
Approximate time	2½ hours
Parking	Selborne village car park
Route terrain	Field and woodland paths, muddy after rain, with a short section of roadside pavement
Dog friendly	Please lead dogs along the road near the start
Ordnance Survey maps	Landranger 186 (Aldershot & Guildford), Explorer 133 (Haslemere & Petersfield)

GPS waypoints	
Start	SU 742 335
A	SU 744 330
B	SU 743 320
C	SU 746 319
D	SU 742 315
E	SU 734 321
F	SU 729 328

After leaving the renowned Hampshire village of Selborne, the walk soon leads away from the busy main road and up into the woods adjoining Noar Hill nature reserve. After continuing around the hillside, the path descends through fields before climbing an old green lane onto the wooded slopes of Selborne Hill. The final descent is made along a narrow zigzag path back into Selborne. It is well worth allowing time at the beginning or end of the walk to wander through the village and visit the museums and church.

Selborne was made famous by the eminent naturalist Gilbert White who was born here in his grandfather's vicarage in 1720. He spent most of his life in the village studying and writing about natural history and wrote the book which has made him internationally well-known, *The Natural History and Antiquities of Selborne*. His old home is now a museum and stands opposite the church of St Mary, built around 1180.

Appropriately, the walk runs close to Noar Hill's ancient chalk quarries, now a nature reserve renowned for its wild flowers and attendant butterflies in summer. Thirty-five species of butterfly have been recorded here. It is also a good site for cowslips, and 11 species of orchid grow here.

Much of the local countryside is now in the hands of the National Trust, including Selborne Common and the zigzag path near the end of the walk. This path was constructed by Gilbert White and his brother in 1753.

Leave the car park by the vehicle entrance beside the **Selborne Arms** pub, and turn right along the main road through the village. Continue down the hill until, just after the turning to Newton Valence, you reach the Gilbert White drinking trough on the right-hand side of the road.

A few paces farther on, turn right through the kissing-gate **A** and follow the signposted footpath through a small patch of woodland into a field. Bear right, and follow the field edge until it turns away to your right; keep ahead here, and pass through the gap in the hedge 100 yds in front of you.

Turn left, and follow the hedge to the far corner of this next field. Zigzag left and right through a gap in the hedges, then follow the cross-field path that rises gently to a metal kissing-gate on the far side of the field. Keep ahead through the gate, and follow the waymarked footpath until you reach a waymark post marking the bridleway junction at the edge of High Wood Hanger **B**.

Turn right onto the bridleway, and continue through the woods to a junction with a wider track. Turn left up the hill, then keep left along the signposted Hangers Way when the track divides at the entrance to Noar Hill nature reserve. Continue the steady climb to a signposted bridleway junction, on your right near the top of the hill **C**.

Turn right here, and continue through a gate into Noar Hill nature reserve. Fork left when the track divides at a bridleway signpost and bench seat, and follow it gently downhill to the next bridleway signpost. Turn left, leaving the main track, and drop down out of

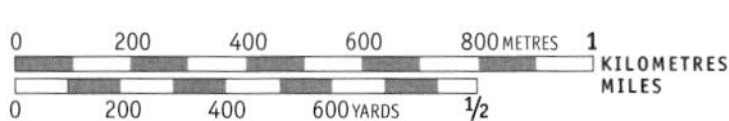

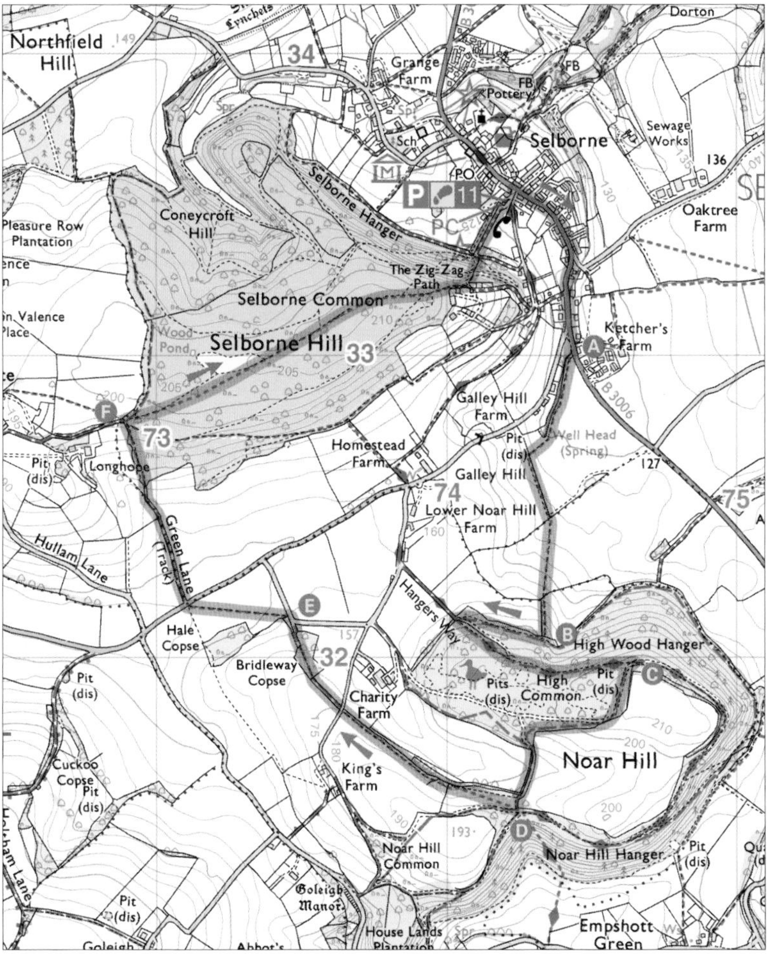

SCALE 1:25 000 or 2½ INCHES to 1 MILE 4CM to 1KM

The decorative Gilbert White fountain at Selborne forms a landmark on this walk

the nature reserve through a wooden pedestrian gate. Cross the shallow valley, and climb to a complex six-way junction **D**.

Turn hard right along the signposted footpath and follow it through the woods until you emerge into a field. Turn right along the field edge, and continue to a tarmac lane. Cross over onto an enclosed bridleway, with pleasant views towards Selborne Hill on your right; soon the path dives through Bridleway Copse, and you reach another tarmac lane **E**.

Turn left, and walk down the lane for 20 yds before turning left at a footpath sign into the adjoining field. Walk diagonally across the field to a gap in the far hedge; cross the road here, and join the bridleway straight ahead. There are glimpses of Longhope on your left as the track climbs through a wooden gate to a crossways; ignore the footpath to Selborne on your right, and keep ahead for another 30 yds.

Turn right at the next crossways **F**, where a broken signpost indicates your route towards Selborne. This broad, confident track leads through the woods and past a clearing on your left; at length, you pass through a gate and continue to a seat at the top of Gilbert White's zigzag path.

Bear left here, and follow the zigzag down through a kissing-gate towards Selborne village. At the foot of the hill, the walk finishes at the car park on your left. ●

Chalk streams at Fullerton

		GPS waypoints
Start	West Down car park, just off the A3057 Stockbridge to Andover road	SU 383 389
Distance	4½ miles (7.3km)	Ⓐ SU 379 396
Height gain	310 feet (95m)	Ⓑ SU 374 395
Approximate time	2½ hours	Ⓒ SU 366 407
Parking	At the start	Ⓓ SU 385 404
Route terrain	Field paths and old railway track	Ⓔ SU 390 400
Dog friendly	Please lead dogs near grazing animals between Ⓒ and Ⓔ	Ⓕ SU 386 394
Ordnance Survey maps	Landranger 185 (Winchester & Basingstoke), Explorer 131 (Romsey, Andover & Test Valley)	

Set around the confluence of two of Hampshire's best-known chalk streams, the walk sets out along the abandoned track of a former railway line. After passing Fullerton Mill, set astride its striking millpond on the River Anton, the route continues through farmland along the Anton Valley. Then it crosses the watershed of Red Hill, drops into the Test Valley, and arrives on the outskirts of Wherwell before meandering back across Chilbolton Cow Common and West Down.

The River Test is probably Britain's most renowned fly-fishing river for trout. The sparklingly clear water allows views of fine flecked and spotted specimens on this walk. The River Anton runs into the Test, close to the start of the walk. It is beside the Anton at Fullerton that the remains of a Roman villa have been discovered, and a section of the mosaic floor now decorates the hall of a local house. Fields beside the river here were once water meadows, and the sluice gates are still evident. An operator, known as a 'drowner', flooded the riverside meadows in winter. This kept the ground temperature up and provided earlier spring grazing the following year.

Leave the car park, cross the road, and follow the Test Way sign down onto the disused railway line. This was the Andover–Romsey line. When you reach the brick railway bridge on your left, turn right along the old line towards Andover. Follow the track, which crosses the Test and then runs through Fullerton Junction where the line divided. The Test Way now runs over the wedge-shaped island platform where trains towards Andover and Whitchurch once departed from the left and right-hand sides. Continue along the old station approach until you reach the A3057 Ⓐ.

Cross this busy main road, turn left, and walk up over the old railway bridge. Keep well into the side and *take care on this short section, especially if walking with children or dogs.* Just after the bridge, turn right onto the

Longstock road. Look out for the picture-postcard view of Fullerton Mill on your left. Bear right towards Red Rice when the road divides and continue uphill as far as the first entrance to Fullerton Manor **B**.

Turn right here up a gravel track and into a field. From here there are wide views of the Anton Valley, and you may also be lucky enough to see roe deer. Bear left along the cart track that runs along the left-hand side of the field, through a space in the hedge at the end and continue straight ahead on the path running down the left-hand side of the following field. Soon the hedge drops away on your left; keep ahead beside the post and wire fence across the centre of a large, open field. On the far side of the field, turn left onto the cart track that runs beside the field edge and continue to a gate across the track, about 300 yds farther on **C**.

Turn right through a kissing-gate and follow the path across a concrete farm bridge, then bear gently right to a wooden footbridge over the main river. Turn left over the bridge, and continue through the woods straight ahead until you reach a footpath sign at the woodland edge. Turn right here, and follow the wooded field edge as far as the A3057.

Cross the road and take the bridleway immediately opposite, continuing through a wooden gate and up Red Hill out of the Anton Valley. Bear right when you come to a wire fence enclosing young trees on your left and carry on through a small wooden gate. Follow the path as it winds up the hill and runs between hedges, finally reaching an open vista at the top of the hill.

The radio telescope on Chilbolton Down lies straight ahead, with Chilbolton church across the valley to your left. Turn left here, and follow the track as it drops down the hill and bears to the right. Pass under the disused railway bridge and out through a gate onto the village road **D**.

Turn left onto the road and follow it for 100 yds. Immediately after the thatched Westmill Cottage, turn right onto the signposted Test Way. Cross the long wooden footbridge over the Test and follow the path across Chilbolton Cow Common.

The priory at Wherwell, close by on the river, stands on the site of an earlier abbey founded in the 10th century by Elfrida. It is said that after her husband, King Edgar, died, she murdered his son. To make amends she built the abbey and ended her life in penance. The priory is the site for another interesting local legend. A tree in the centre of the lawn was blown down, and a man's body was found buried beneath the roots and covered

Alongside the crystal-clear running water of a Hampshire chalk river

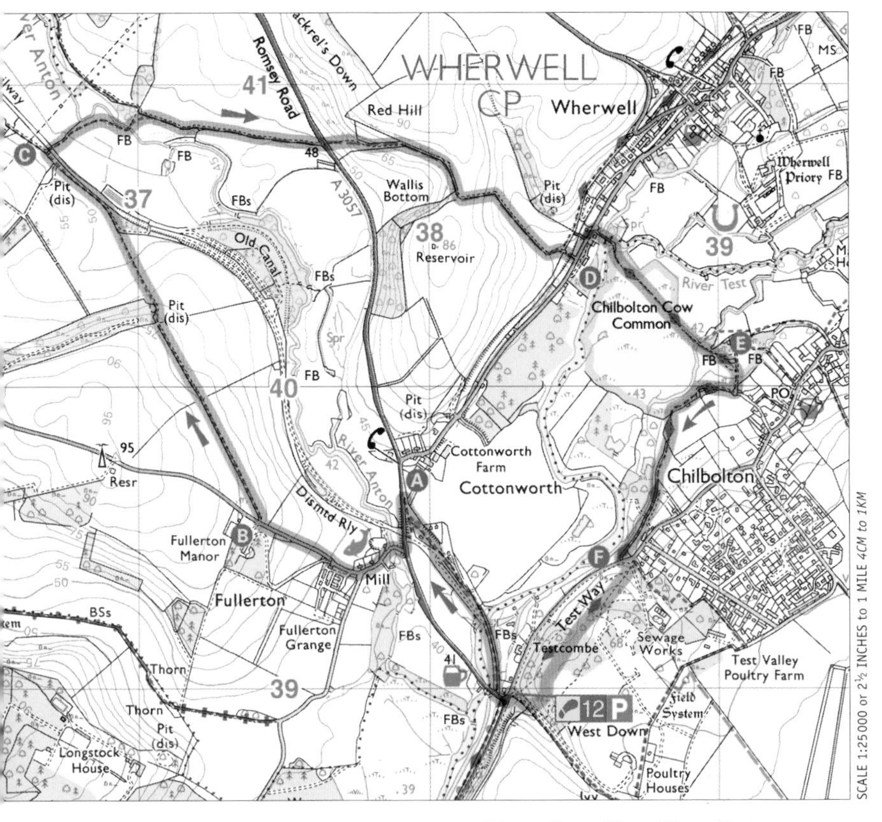

by a hurdle. It is also said that a great treasure is buried here but that sudden death will be the reward for anyone who tries to recover it.

On the far side of the common a small footbridge takes you across a carrier of the Test and, 175 yds farther on, you'll reach a small car park and gravel track **E**.

Turn right here, then right again at the cattle-grid. *Alternatively, turn left over the cattle-grid to visit the* **Abbot's Mitre** *pub in Chilbolton.*

Take the track around the edge of the common until you reach the gate leading into the Memorial Playing Field. Keep right here, following the waymarked Test Way as it weaves its way along a narrow path and across a corner of the playing field. Finally the path runs between fences and emerges onto the village road at a small green with a seat **F**.

Turn left onto the road and then almost immediately right, following the green Test Way arrow that points up the concrete access road to West Down. A few paces farther on, turn off to your right through a kissing-gate, and follow the grassy track gently uphill. Bear left, then right, near the summit, and continue into the woods through a second kissing-gate. Keep straight on here, following the route marked by substantial red posts. Pass a concrete road on your left, and carry on beside a large clearing on your left. On the far side of the clearing fork right at the red 'SES Endurance' waymark post. Now follow the path through a kissing-gate and down a steep bank back to the car park.

East Meon and the Downs

Start	Workhouse Lane car park on the western edge of the village
Distance	4¾ miles (7.8km)
Height gain	605 feet (185m)
Approximate time	2½ hours
Parking	At the start
Route terrain	Field edge paths and country tracks that will be muddy after rain
Dog friendly	Dogs must be led near farm animals and on short sections of road
Ordnance Survey maps	Landranger 185 (Winchester & Basingstoke), Explorer 132 (Winchester)

GPS waypoints

Start	SU 677 222
A	SU 677 211
B	SU 673 201
C	SU 666 210
D	SU 668 232
E	SU 677 225

The thriving community of East Meon lies just off the South Downs Way and close to the source of the River Meon. This route strikes out through farmland before a steep climb up onto Small Down, which rewards your efforts with a spectacular downland panorama. An easy descent along the National Trail leads to the hamlet of Drayton, where the walk returns across farmland to East Meon.

This is an area with a violent past. The river takes its name from the Meonwaras, a tribe of Jutish invaders who settled the valley in pre-Saxon times. Daily life in East Meon dates from about this period, though the church was not built until soon after the Norman Conquest. Its black marble font lost its lead lining during the English civil war, when a Roundhead army stole it to make bullets before the Battle of Cheriton in 1644. Today the area is rather more peaceful, and East Meon welcomes visitors with a shop, post office and two pubs, **The Izaak Walton** and **Ye Old George**.

Leave the car park, take the signposted footpath to the left of the wooden sports pavilion and walk across the green. Go through the gap between the houses, bear right into Duncombe Road, and keep ahead to the T-junction. Turn left, pass the houses of Coombe Road Terrace, and turn right onto the signposted footpath through a small parking area and a kissing-gate. Bear slightly left across the field towards the kissing-gate at the right-hand end of a line of trees on the horizon.

Keep ahead, following the waymarked footpath along the left-hand hedge until it bends away to your left. Bear right here, striking out across the field to a signpost in the valley bottom. Keep ahead along the winding edge of the next field with the hedge on your left, and continue to a stile **A** as the woods close in from your right.

Nip across, turn right, and walk up the short hill to a metal gate. Turn left through the gate and follow the left-hand field edge to reach a three-way signpost in the hedge, just before the gate leading out of the field. Turn right for the steep climb up onto Small Down, aiming for the stile to the right of a small clump of fir trees, where the view will reward your efforts. Cross the stile and keep ahead beside the wire fence on your left to a metal gate at the summit of the Down.

Turn left through the gate and follow the grassy ridge towards the masts on the skyline, as far as a second gate and waymark post. Turn right through the gate, then bear left around the end of

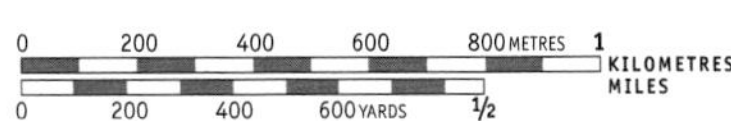

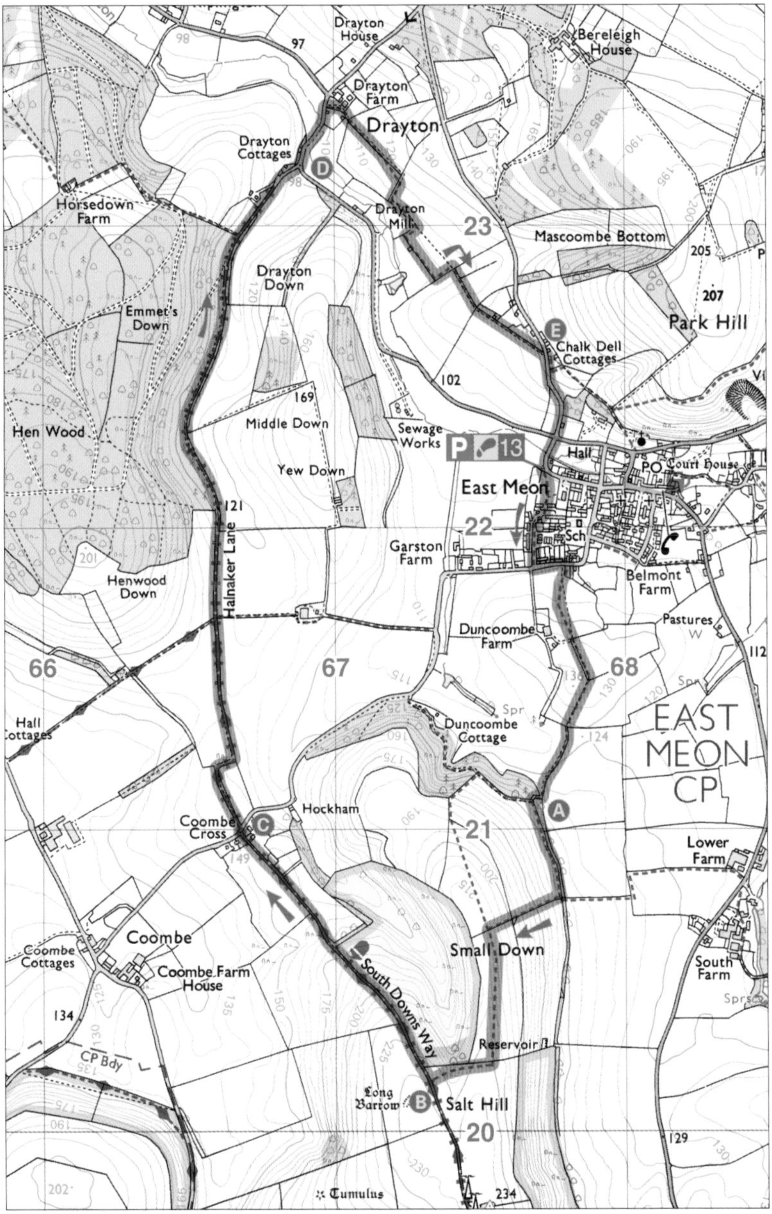

SCALE 1:25 000 or 2½ INCHES to 1 MILE *4CM to 1KM*

View from Small Down

the woods and through the valley to a stile and South Downs Way signpost **B**.

Jump the stile, turn right onto the South Downs Way, and follow it off the Down along a tree-shaded sunken way.

Zigzag right and left across the lane at Coombe Cross **C**, following the South Downs Way past a wooden barrier. The track makes a double bend and continues past a crossways where the South Downs Way turns off to the left. Keep ahead along the signposted byway as it slips through the valley along the edge of Hen Wood. A pair of metal barriers heralds the end of the woodland and soon the route continues along a lane to meet a road at a grassy triangle **D**.

Turn left along the road for 200 yds; then, just before the junction at Drayton Farm, turn right along a narrow signposted footpath. Cross a stile, then keep ahead through a metal field gate and walk beside the hedge on your right, continuing through a second gate to a waymarked stile. Nip across and turn right, following the hedge as it winds along the boundary of a large field. The path bends left in the far corner of the field and, after 75 yds, you'll come to a stile and gate on your right.

Turn right over the stile and follow the fence on your left to a second stile and gate. Keep ahead beside the hedge to a final stile and gate, where the path meets the road opposite Chalk Dell Cottages **E**.

Turn right onto the road and drop down to the crossroads. Keep ahead along Workhouse Lane towards the car park and village hall to reach the car park entrance on your right. ●

Standing Hat, New Forest

Start	Standing Hat car park, Brockenhurst. Up gravel track behind Balmer Lawn Hotel
Distance	5 miles (8km)
Height gain	150 feet (45m)
Approximate time	2½ hours
Parking	At the start
Route terrain	All-weather forest tracks
Dog friendly	Dogs must be led near grazing animals
Ordnance Survey maps	Landranger 196 (The Solent & Isle of Wight), Explorer OL22 (New Forest)

GPS waypoints

- SU 314 036
- Ⓐ SU 321 040
- Ⓑ SU 321 043
- Ⓒ SU 320 050
- Ⓓ SU 328 057
- Ⓔ SU 333 058
- Ⓕ SU 332 047
- Ⓖ SU 335 037
- Ⓗ SU 316 035

The intriguing name of this easy to follow woodland walk reflects the local New Forest term 'Hat' or 'Hatt', meaning a small hill topped with trees. The route uses all-weather gravel tracks to explore the attractive Inclosures between Lyndhurst and Brockenhurst, setting out through mixed woodland with oak, birch and beech trees supplementing the conifers. In summer, the scent of bracken hangs in the air and spectacular displays of foxgloves fringe the forest rides. The walk passes a ride named in memory of the naturalist F W Frohawk, renowned for his butterfly recording work in the New Forest. You'll find some appealing informal picnic spots close to the halfway point, before returning past the historic Victoria Tilery Cottage.

These woods are home to the tiny roe deer and the tall, slender fallow, the most common deer of the New Forest. Woodpeckers of all three types can be seen here and, as dusk approaches, a tawny owl may fly silently overhead, calling to its youngsters, or a woodcock may fly low across your path.

Turn left out of the car park, go through the pedestrian gate and fork immediately right along the gravelled forest track. Ignore all minor turnings and continue along the main gravelled ride until it bears sharp left where a smaller grassy ride continues straight ahead Ⓐ.

Bear left here, continuing along the main ride as it curves gently to the right and climbs to a waymarked crossroads with another gravelled ride Ⓑ.

Turn left, following the waymarked route towards Lyndhurst. The trail winds gently uphill and the woods close in as you drop down again to a T-junction with another ride Ⓒ.

The Lyndhurst trail turns off to the left here, but your way lies to the right. The gravelled track climbs gently for

200 yds and reaches a fork with another similar track.

Behind the wooden fence on your left, the grassy Frohawk Ride commemorates the work of the Norfolk naturalist Frederick Frohawk. Born in 1861, Frohawk made regular summer visits to the New Forest in search of butterflies. His wife Mabel often came with him, as well as his daughter Valezina, who was named after a variety of the silver-washed fritillary. This is one of our largest butterflies and it flies in July and August. Another rare species, the pearl-bordered fritillary, can be seen feeding in the Frohawk Ride in May and June.

Fork right here. Ignore all turnings and simply follow the main track as it climbs steadily to the wooden gates that mark the boundary of Parkhill Inclosure **D**.

Go through the gates into Denny Wood and follow the track as it bears steadily around to the right; the attractive clearings in this area are perfect for a leisurely informal picnic. Soon the track swings back to the left and reaches a wooden barrier at a T-junction with the private drive to Denny Lodge **E**.

Turn right onto the drive; then, 200 yds farther on, fork left off the tarmac along the waymarked gravel cycle track. Drop down the hill past Denny Cottage on your left and, after a further 100 yards, keep straight on when a gravelled track turns off to your right. Continue through the wooden gate into Stubby Copse Inclosure, still following the waymarked cycle route. Stick with the track as it bears to the left and climbs gently to a turning on your left **F**.

Keep straight on along the waymarked route, and continue past another cycle route that turns off to your right. Now the track bears to the right and drops gently towards a gravel crossroads about 100 yds before a set of wooden gates across the track **G**. Turn right onto a long, straight section. Just over ½ mile farther on, go straight across at a waymarked cycle track crossroads. Continue over the Etherise Gutter and bear left, still following the gravel track where a grassy ride

Roe deer kids – often twins – are hidden in undergrowth by their mother while she feeds

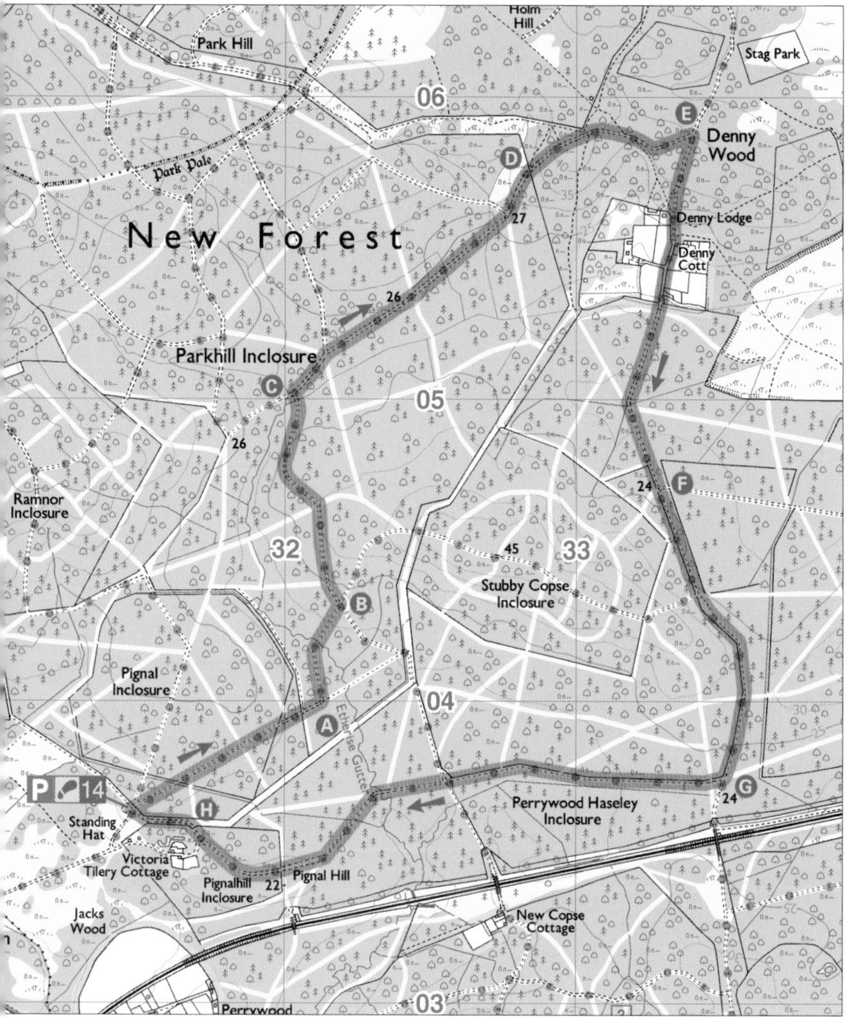

SCALE 1:25000 or $2\frac{1}{2}$ INCHES to 1 MILE *4CM to 1KM*

continues straight ahead. Now the trail curves back to the right, and your way is barred by a set of wooden Inclosure gates across the track.

Hidden in the woods on your left at this point, the Victoria Tilery Cottage offers an interesting insight into life and property values in the mid-19th century. As part of the deal for its line through the New Forest, the Southampton and Dorchester Railway Company established a £12,000 compensation fund to finance drainage projects in the open forest. The Victoria Brick and Tile Works was founded at

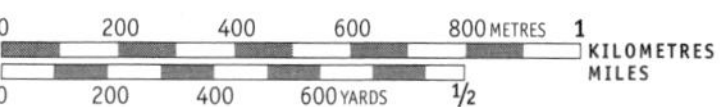

Pignal Hill at about the same time, and supplied some of the tiles used in this work. The company's accounts include reference to a cottage built by a Mr Waterman in the late 1840s for a cost of just £40. This may be the former manager's bungalow, now known as the Victoria Tilery Cottage.

Go through the pedestrian gate **H** and follow the track around to the left for the last 220 yds back to the car park. ●

Fritham and Ashley Walk

Start	Fritham village – best approached from the B3078 Brook to Godshill Road, due to limited access from the A31
Distance	5¼ miles (8.5km)
Height gain	310 feet (95m)
Approximate time	2½ hours
Parking	Forestry Commission car park just beyond the Royal Oak
Route terrain	All-weather forest tracks
Dog friendly	Dogs must be led near grazing animals
Ordnance Survey maps	Landranger 195 (Bournemouth & Purbeck), Explorer OL22 (New Forest)

GPS waypoints

Start	SU 231 141
A	SU 222 142
B	SU 208 141
C	SU 202 141
D	SU 193 135
E	SU 197 130
F	SU 203 129
G	SU 206 127
H	SU 218 131

This relatively remote walk offers a mixture of heath and woodland scenery, with some good views across the varied New Forest landscape. Glimpses of Eyeworth Lodge recall its former links with gunpowder manufacturing, and the distinctive black factory letterbox still stands close to the start of the walk. The route also skirts the Ashley Walk bombing range, testing ground for the famous 'Dam Buster' bouncing bombs used by the RAF during the Second World War.

In the mid-1970s one of these bombs was reconstructed from sections salvaged from Ashley Walk and presented to the RAF's 617 'Dam Buster' Squadron. Sir Barnes Wallis, who designed the bomb, attended the ceremony at Middle Wallop air base near Andover. Ashley Walk was the test bed for a wide variety of other military hardware, including the largest bomb ever to be dropped in England – the 22,000-pound 'Grand Slam', also designed by Sir Barnes Wallis.

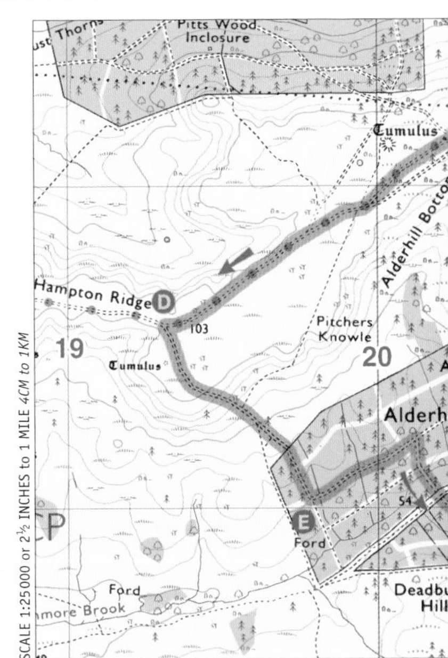

Walk back towards the car park entrance and, before reaching the road, turn left onto a gravel track waymarked 'Cycle route to Frogham only'. Keep to the track as it runs downhill through

Ashley Walk hut, Fritham

Gorley Bushes, with glimpses of Eyeworth Lodge across the lawn on your right-hand side.

Originally built as a hunting lodge, this large redbrick house became the headquarters of a small gunpowder factory in 1859. Ten years later the business was bought out by the Schultze Gunpowder Company, which began making powder for the Franco-German war. The factory went on to supply smokeless powder for sportsmen and, later on, gunpowder made here was used in the First World War. The business relied on local supplies of sulphur, saltpetre and charcoal, and constructed the nearby Eyeworth pond to provide a water supply.

Fork left at the foot of the hill Ⓐ, follow the waymarked gravel cycle route as it swings right over the Latchmoor Brook, and fork left 50 yds after the bridge. Now the track crosses a small brook, swings hard right at the next fork, and begins the climb towards Ashley Cross. Continue uphill past a five-bar gate on your left, until you reach a waymarked fork with a second five-bar gate on your left and a clump of holly trees on the right Ⓑ.

The forester's cottage that once stood behind this gate was destroyed during the Second World War, when the Ashley

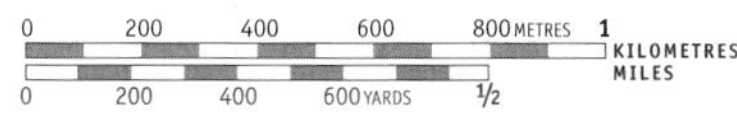

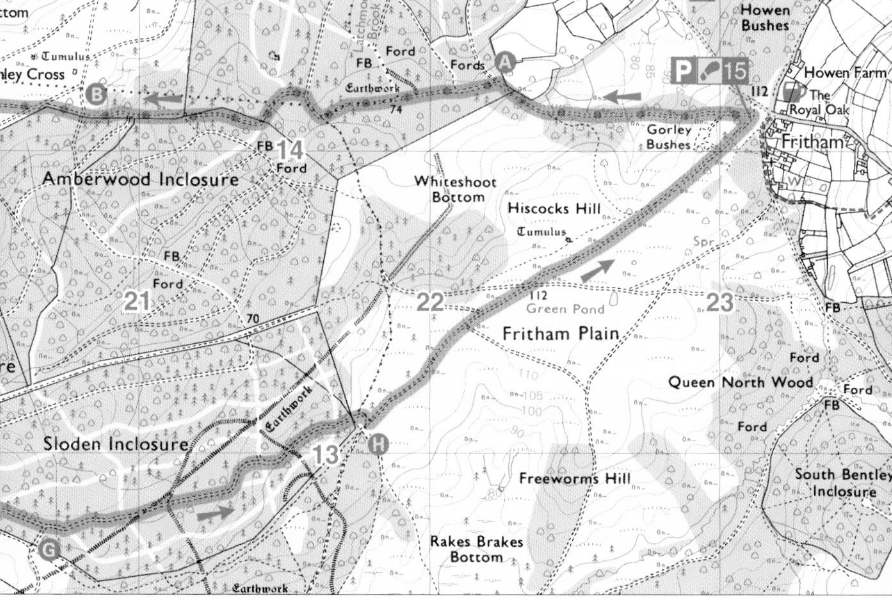

Royal Oak, Fritham

Walk bombing range encompassed some 4,000 acres of heathland. Inside its nine-mile perimeter fence, the site was a maze of natural and man-made targets that included bunkers, trenches and steel plates, as well as two massive concrete walls at Cockley Plain and Leaden Hall. Over 400 craters were counted on aerial photos taken after the range closed in 1946 – but, more than half a century later, there's little left to see. The little brick and concrete observation hut away to your right is now the only wartime building left standing on the former Ashley Walk range.

Keep straight on beside the wire fence on your left and continue ahead along the gravel track as the edge of Amberwood Inclosure drops away on your left.

When the track divides C, take the waymarked left-hand fork to the left of the mound; this easy stretch along the top of Hampton Ridge offers good views on both sides. Continue until the track bends to the right, just over ½ mile farther on D.

Turn sharp left onto a lesser-used gravel track and keep ahead past a lone birch tree. The track bears to the left and drops into the valley, before diving through a gate into Alderhill Inclosure and dropping gently down to a cross-ways E. Turn left here, walk to an indistinct green crossways, and continue for a further 50 yds. Now turn hard right, and follow the gravel track down to a substantial bridge over the Latchmoor Brook. Keep ahead through two gates as you cross the wide grass track that divides Alderhill and Sloden Inclosures, and then continue until the track divides and a path goes off to the left F.

Go straight on up the gentle hill until you reach a junction where a track goes off to the right G and leaves the inclosure through a gate.

Bear slightly to the left and continue through the wood. This gravel track snakes up the hill and finally leaves the inclosure through a gate. Here, the track bears around to the right and brings you to a T-junction H.

Turn left. From here, it's fast, easy walking along the well-made level track across Fritham Plain. After about a mile you'll come to some bushes and a forest barrier; continue straight ahead, back into the car park with **the Royal Oak** pub just beyond. ●

Brockenhurst Park and Roydon Woods

		GPS waypoints
Start	Ivy Wood car park; B3055 just east of Brockenhurst	SU 315 025
Distance	5¼ miles (8.3km)	Ⓐ SU 314 025
Height gain	345 feet (105m)	Ⓑ SU 304 021
Approximate time	2½ hours	Ⓒ SU 306 015
Parking	At the start	Ⓓ SU 313 004
Route terrain	Mainly forest tracks and paths, with some serious mud in wet conditions	Ⓔ SU 315 002 Ⓕ SU 330 008 Ⓖ SU 331 015 Ⓗ SU 324 014 Ⓙ SU 320 022
Dog friendly	Dogs must be led in Brockenhurst Park, and on the short stretches of minor road	
Ordnance Survey maps	Landranger 196 (The Solent & Isle of Wight), Explorer OL22 (New Forest)	

This walk goes via a country lane to Brockenhurst's tiny old historic church. It then passes through a woodland nature reserve out onto farmland and returns through ancient New Forest woodland finally to take a track alongside the Lymington River in Ivy Wood, renowned for its wonderful display of spring flowers – mainly primroses, violets and wood anemones. Some paths may be muddy after wet weather.

Allow extra time on this walk to visit the forest church passed on the route. St Nicholas' Church stands on a mound away from Brockenhurst village and surrounded by fields and forest. It is the oldest church in the New Forest and mentioned in William I's *Domesday Book*. This small church, with its musicians gallery, has a Norman archway over the south door and tall, narrow 13th-century arches containing later windows of stained glass flowers. In one wall a part of the masonry is very early – from 5th or 6th century.

Face the car park entrance and turn into the woods on your left, almost opposite the substantial 'Ivy Wood' car park name board. An indistinct forest path drops gently towards the young Lymington River and runs beside the water to a road junction opposite the entrance to **Whitley Ridge Hotel** Ⓐ.

Turn left towards Brockenhurst, cross the river by the bridge, and follow Mill Lane for 350 yds to a house on your right called Longbow. Turn left here through a kissing-gate opposite the house, then bear right to follow the hedge on your right. Cross a couple of stiles, and continue to a kissing-gate on your right, where the path rejoins Mill Lane. Bear left past North Lodge, and continue for 50 yds.

Turn left up the gravel track Ⓑ

between Reynolds Cottage and Mulberry Cottage and climb the hill, past the entrance to St Nicholas' churchyard, to a small parking area at the junction with Church Lane. It is well worth taking a slight detour through the churchyard. To the left of the church entrance is a yew tree reputed to be at least 1,000 years old. The graveyard has two memorials of special interest. Brusher Mills, is buried here, and his gravestone depicts his colourful life. This Victorian character is seen outside the charcoal burner's hut where he lived for around 30 years, holding a handful of snakes. During his life he caught thousands of snakes in the forest, some of which went to zoos to feed other snakes, and some were sold for their skins or fat. Now numbers are much depleted, and all British snakes are protected by law.

Close to Brusher Mills' grave, and on the north side of the churchyard, is a memorial to the New Zealand soldiers who died at a nearby hospital for the seriously wounded during the First World War. Brockenhurst also had numbers of wounded Indian soldiers quartered there, and one road, Meerut Road, is named in their memory.

Turn left along Church Lane for 250 yds; just beyond the right-hand bend, you'll see a signposted bridleway C opposite the drive to Beech Tree Cottage.

Turn left here, and follow the bridleway south. Shortly, you will see an avenue of trees that runs across the path in each direction. Known locally as the Gallops, this avenue was used for training racehorses. *Thatched Cottage,* which won a Grand National in the 1950s, was one of a number trained here. This was also the site of the hospital for New Zealand wounded mentioned before. Continue along the track and through a gate into Roydon Woods nature reserve. If you are lucky, you may catch sight of one of the three kinds of deer that can be found in these woods: sika, fallow and roe. The track runs up and down in a gentle switchback through the woods and climbs to a second wooden gate; 200 yds farther on, you'll come to a signposted bridleway junction with a wider gravel track D.

Turn left here, and bear right when the track to Roydon Manor House forks off to the left. Continue down the hill until you

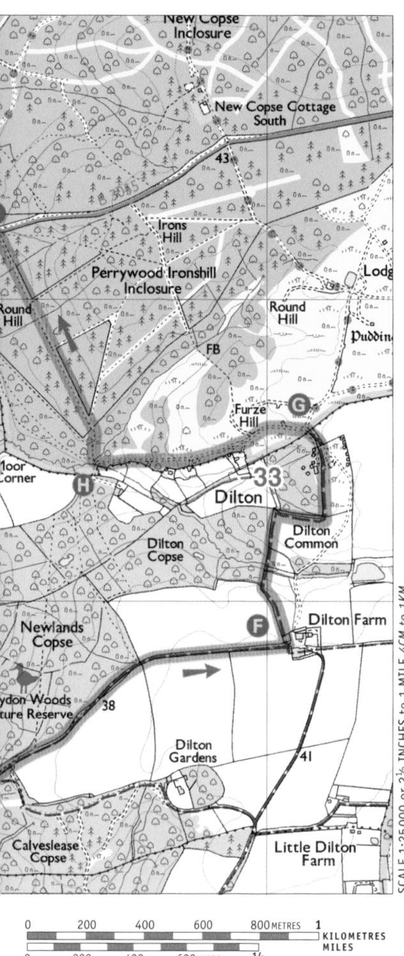

reach a gate on the left with a prominent orange and white metal marker post **E**.

Turn left here through the gate onto a bridleway. This wooded track gives good views of Roydon Manor on the left, the present home of the Morant family. It was also for some years the home of the author and naturalist W H Hudson at the end of the 19th century. He wrote *Hampshire Days* while he was here. The path drops gently down to cross the Lymington River on a wooden footbridge, then climbs again past a bridleway turning on the right. Keep straight on here along the woodland edge, finally leaving the nature reserve at a metal farm gate. Continue along the wide farm track ahead of you, as far as the buildings at Dilton Farm **F**; this section may be muddy in wet weather.

Turn left here and follow the waymarked bridleway between wire fences. The track drops to a stream crossing, then rises to regain the lost height. Follow the track as it swings first right, then left, and continue past a ramshackle collection of farm buildings and old Nissen huts. Here the track zigzags right and left at a wooden bridleway signpost, and runs for 70 yds to meet a wider concrete track at a metal farm gate **G**.

Turn left here, following the track as it runs downhill past houses on your left to the confluence of two small streams **H**.

Here the main track veers off across the stream to the left; your way, however, lies across the smaller stream to your right, on a narrow path uphill through the woods. After about 150 yds the path bears left between wooden gateposts into Perrywood Ironshill Inclosure. Thirty yards past the gateposts, take the left-hand fork along a grassy forest ride through the conifer plantation. Continue straight ahead, ignoring a turning on the right, until the ride comes to an abrupt end; now carry straight on along a narrow woodland path until you can see the B3055 about 40 yds ahead. Turn left here onto a similar path, and walk through to a small clearing **J** separated from the road by a low wooden barrier.

With the barrier on your right, follow the indistinct path that drops down through the trees to the river, about 90 yds ahead. Turn right, and follow the riverside path over a series of small plank bridges for about 300 yds. Now turn right again for the final short stretch back to the car park. ●

Queen Elizabeth Country Park

Start	Queen Elizabeth Country Park visitor centre, off the A3 south of Petersfield
Distance	Woodland loop: 3 miles (5km) / Butser Hill loop: 2½ miles (4km)
Height gain	Woodland loop: 510 feet (155m) Butser Hill: 525 feet (160m)
Approximate time	3 hours(each loop 1½ hours)
Parking	Pay and Display car park at the start
Route terrain	Broad woodland tracks (muddy in places) on the woodland loop, with grassy downland paths on Butser Hill
Dog friendly	Dogs are welcome under close control or on a lead – there is a large deer population in the woods, with grazing sheep on Butser Hill
Ordnance Survey maps	Landranger 197 (Chichester & the South Downs), Explorer 120 (Chichester)

GPS waypoints

- Start: SU 718 185
- A SU 718 181
- B SU 729 193
- C SU 727 199
- D SU 723 191
- E SU 720 189
- F SU 716 188
- G SU 716 203
- H SU 717 199
- J SU 718 192

Queen Elizabeth Country Park straddles the A3 south of Petersfield, and this walk makes the most of its two very different faces. To the east, the gentler woodland loop follows well-made tracks through the native beech and conifer plantations of Queen Elizabeth Forest. West of the road, a stiff climb up the grassy slopes of Butser Hill is rewarded by a stunning 360-degree panorama from the highest point on the South Downs. You are advised not to attempt this section in poor visibility.

Both routes start from the welcoming visitor centre, where you'll find information and a shop as well as a nice **café**, **picnic area** and toilets.

Woodland loop

Face the large rustic signpost just to the left of the visitor centre entrance, and turn right onto the waymarked South Downs Way. Pass the café courtyard, the pond and picnic area, and continue to a country park road A.

Zigzag left and right across the road, then fork left beyond the wooden barrier to follow the signposted South Downs Way walkers' route along a gravelled path. Stick with the South Downs Way (SDW) when it briefly joins a park road, passes through the small Benham Bushes car park, and continues as a gravelled forest track. Keep ahead past the barbecue shelter on your right, and stay

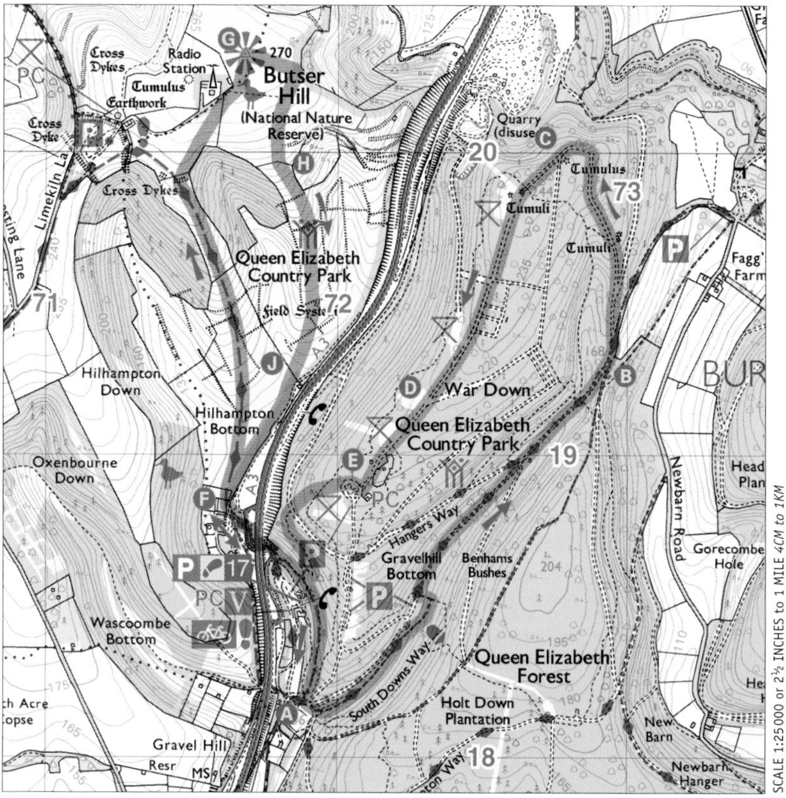

SCALE 1:25 000 or 2½ INCHES to 1 MILE *4CM to 1KM*

on the main track as it climbs gently to a junction where the SDW walkers' route joins the SDW bridleway B.

Keep ahead for 90 yds, then fork left off the SDW onto a track way-marked with a red bootprint. Fork left again after 150 yds along a good forest track, still following the red bootprints that will guide you back to the car park. The track continues to climb, then bends left and levels off at a fork C.

Fork right as the track climbs again briefly to its summit at a clearing on your right. Now this woodland track takes on a more open feel, with occasional clearings, bench seats and glimpses across the valley towards Butser Hill on your right.

Keep ahead past the clearing at War Down, where another track trails in from your left D, and drop steadily down to the Juniper car park E.

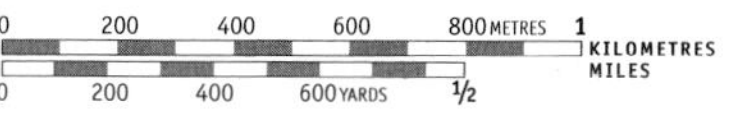

Fork right at the car park, following the red boot waymarks into the trees and dropping downhill on a narrow woodland path. Cross a wider track and continue downhill, with views of the A3 racing through the valley below. Now the path clings to the hillside and zigzags down beside a wooden fence to the main visitor centre car park where your walk began.

Butser Hill loop

Face the large rustic signpost as before, but this time turn left along the waymarked South Downs Way (SDW) and follow it back to the car park entrance and through the tunnel under the A3. Turn left across the park access road, watching out for traffic entering from the A3, and continue through the barbecue parking area. Join the gravelled path marked by blue SDW bridleway posts and walk to the gate at the foot of the Downs **F**.

As you follow the well-worn path up the slope towards the radio station mast, look out for the banks defining the boundaries of the fields laid out by early settlers. Stone Age flint tools have been found in the area, and there are Bronze Age burial mounds and cross-dykes on the hill's eastern slopes. In summer, the slopes of the hill are clothed in wild flowers.

Go through a wooden gate, and continue up the hill. Bear gently to the right, parallel with a wire fence, when you reach a parting of the ways. Then, bear right along the higher of two green tracks as the fence bends away right, heading just to the right of the radio mast. Keep ahead for a few paces past the mast enclosure, then bear left to the distinctive concrete Ordnance Survey pillar on the very top of the hill **G**.

From here, the spectacular views extend across Portsmouth and the Solent to the Isle of Wight. Closer to home, look out for the conical thatched roofs of the roundhouses at Butser Ancient Farm, which lies east of the A3 and a couple of miles south of your vantage point.

Turn right along a grassy path, with the line of the Downs ahead of you. Cross another path, then turn hard right when you reach the fence enclosing some thick bushes. Continue for 120 yds with the radio mast on your right and the A3 cutting through the valley on your left. Then, fork right along a narrower path heading directly along the line of the A3 until you reach a stile and gate **H**.

Cross over and keep ahead as the path drops steeply down, bearing very gently right to reach a stile **J** by a small pond in the valley bottom.

Cross the stile, and walk parallel with the A3 to rejoin your outward route at the gate **F**. Now, simply retrace your outward steps under the A3 and back to the visitor centre. ●

Butser Hill

Chilcomb and the South Downs

Start	Cheesefoot Head, on the A272 east of Winchester
Distance	$6\frac{1}{4}$ miles (10km)
Height gain	690 feet (210m)
Approximate time	3 hours
Parking	Hampshire County Council car park at the start
Route terrain	Easy to follow bridleways, muddy in places, and short lengths of minor road. The route crosses a live MOD firing range near Chilcomb, and *this path must not be used when the red flags are flying.* Before setting out, tel: 01962 853663 to check for closures and firing dates
Dog friendly	Dogs must be led on the short sections of public road, and through the firing range
Ordnance Survey maps	Landranger 185 (Winchester & Basingstoke), Explorer 132 (Winchester)

GPS waypoints

- Start: SU 529 277
- A: SU 527 277
- B: SU 512 259
- C: SU 503 252
- D: SU 495 267
- E: SU 507 281
- F: SU 513 278

Big skies and easy walking are the ingredients of this downland route, which explores the western fringe of the South Downs National Park. There are dramatic views right from the start as you traverse Fawley Down, before crossing the old Roman road from Winchester to the coast. Continuing through the site of a First World War transit camp you pass through a modern MOD firing range, then join the South Downs Way at the secluded village of Chilcomb with its attractive early Norman church.

Despite its setting less than a mile from the M3 motorway and the busy A31, Chilcomb seems oddly unaffected by the bustle of modern life. Maybe that's because it lies in a fold of the Downs at the end of a no through road, disturbed only by the passage of walkers and cyclists on the South Downs Way. King Cynegils of Wessex gave the Manor of Chilcomb to the church in 636, though it was almost three centuries before Edward the Elder confirmed the gift in a Royal Charter of 908. The original document is in the British Museum, but you can see a Victorian copy in St Andrew's Church, which itself dates from 1060.

(Start) Turn right out of the car park and follow the roadside verge for 80 yds to the South Downs Way crossing. Cross this busy road with care, turn left onto the signposted bridleway, and follow it for 140 yds to a crossways **A**. The South Downs Way turns off to the right here, but your way lies straight ahead through the gap in the wire fence, following the clear green track along the crest of the ridge. This is easy walking, with time to enjoy the long views towards Calshot and the Isle of Wight. The waymarked route joins a farm track as it skirts to the left of a small woodland, then runs between tall hedges until it matures into a tarmac lane at Hydes Cottages B.

Keep ahead here, following Fawley Lane to a crossroads with Morestead Road. Cross with care and keep ahead down Hazeley Road towards Twyford waterworks. Walk over a low summit, pass the drive to Hazeley Down House, and continue as far as the road junction on your left C. To the right, Hazeley Down was formerly the site of a vast First World War transit camp for troops on their way to the battlefields of the Western Front. A century later there's little left to see, apart from a fine memorial to six Battalions of the London Regiment that were stationed here in 1916–17. The memorial stands on private ground, but you can glimpse it from the Pilgrims' Trail or – for a much better view – continue down the road for a couple of hundred yards and look back up to your right.

Turn right onto the Pilgrims' Trail, go through a metal gate, and follow the hedge on your left to a second gate, where the waymarked bridleway zigzags left and right across a farm track. Follow the left-hand field boundary until, at the crest of the hill, the bridleway runs between fences and drops down through woodland to a crossways D.

Turn right, and climb up through the valley beside the woods on your right until the bridleway reaches the Morestead Road. Cross with care to the metal gate at the entrance to the MOD

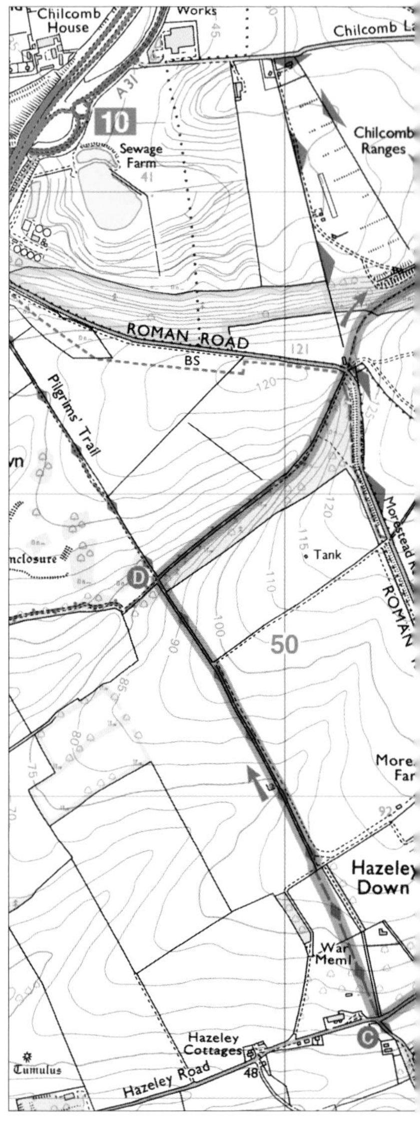

firing range. *You must not go through the range if a red flag indicates that firing is in progress – ring 01962 853663 for advice.* Otherwise, continue through the gate and bear left to the sentry box and flagpole. Now bear right across the field, heading gently downhill on the narrow cross-field path that soon continues as an ancient, well-defined path through the woods. Carry on until you reach the metal gate that heralds St Andrew's churchyard, join

the village lane, and walk down the hill until the lane bends sharp left Ⓔ at a colour-washed cottage on your right.

Turn right here, following the sign-posted footpath in front of the cottages and along an enclosed path that soon bends left and meets a road by a tele-phone box. Turn right along the road, and climb steadily through a double bend to a South Downs Way signpost where the road ends at Little Golders Ⓕ.

Turn left onto the South Downs Way, which follows a hedged track to a three-way signpost. Turn right, walking beside the hedge on your right along the edge of an open field. Simply follow this field boundary as the path winds its way over Telegraph Hill, before diving briefly through a few small wooded areas to reach the crossways that you passed at the beginning of your walk Ⓐ.

Turn left, and retrace your outward steps to the car park just across the A272. ●

Hillhead and Titchfield

Start	The 'Hove-to' car park, on the coast road adjacent to the Hill Head Sailing Club
Distance	6½ miles (10.5km)
Height gain	n/a
Approximate time	3 hours
Parking	At the start
Route terrain	Old canal towpath, farm tracks, village streets and coast path; muddy in places in wet weather
Dog friendly	Dogs should be led in Titchfield, on the coast road, and near farm animals
Ordnance Survey maps	Landranger 196 (The Solent & Isle of Wight), Explorer 119 (Meon Valley, Portsmouth, Gosport & Fareham)

GPS waypoints

Start	SU 535 023
A	SU 530 024
B	SU 532 027
C	SU 541 055
D	SU 535 051
E	SU 527 051
F	SU 523 039
G	SU 517 034

From the breezy harbour at Hill Head this route heads along the coast and skirts Titchfield Haven nature reserve, an important winter refuge for wildfowl as well as a breeding ground for rare avocets. Turning inland past the remains of a former sea lock, the walk follows the disused 17th-century canal all the way into the village of Titchfield – where, perhaps, you might stop for lunch or a welcome cup of coffee. Now the route follows a farm track back to the coast for an exhilarating cliff-top finale with views to the Isle of Wight.

Built by the third Earl of Southampton in 1610, the Titchfield canal is England's second oldest artificial waterway. Before that time ships had reached Titchfield from the coast via the River Meon, but this route was blocked after the Earl constructed a sea wall across the estuary to reclaim the salt marshes for grazing. The boats would have served Titchfield's corn mill and tannery, as well as the ironworks at nearby Funtley. Nevertheless it seems that the canal was not a great success. Within 100 years it had become redundant, and its fate was effectively sealed after the three-arch bridge was built across the mouth of the sea lock.

(Start) Leave the car park by the vehicle entrance and turn left along the pavement. Pass the Visitor Centre, cross the harbour bridge, then dodge left and walk along the sea wall as far as the public toilets at Meon Shore **A**.

Cross the road and turn left through the kissing-gate into Titchfield Haven nature reserve. Follow the path as it bears right, parallel with the road, until the road bends away to the left at Meon Marsh sea lock **B**.

Zigzag left and right over a stile to continue beside the Titchfield canal, with good views across the nature

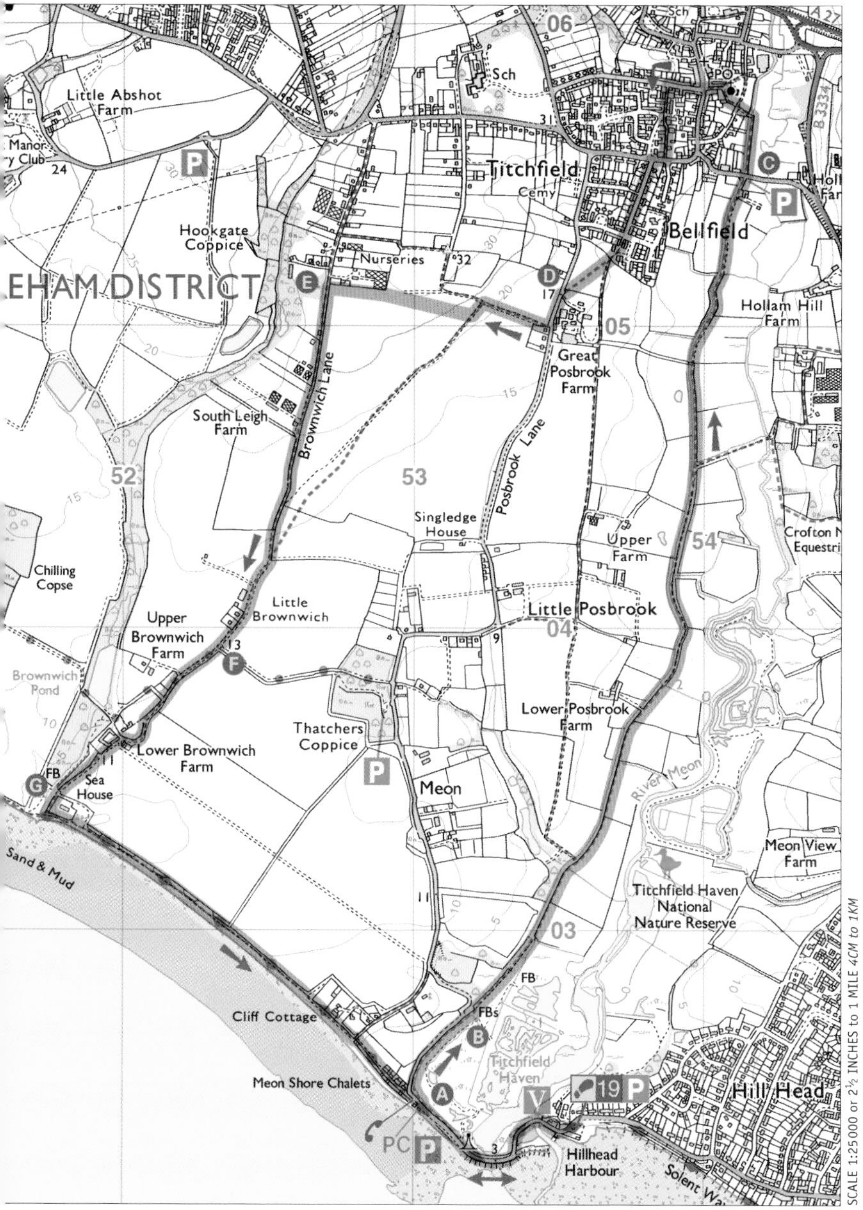

SCALE 1:25 000 or 2½ INCHES to 1 MILE *4CM to 1KM*

reserve on your right. After about 1½ miles the path becomes paved and swings off over a bridge on the left towards Great Posbrook Farm. Keep ahead here through a kissing-gate as the houses at Bellfield come into view across the canal on your left. Continue through two more gates to reach a road by a small car park on your right **C**.

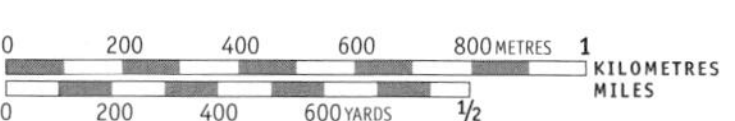

Cross the road and continue beside the canal for a short distance, then follow the path as it swings left over a footbridge and leads past St Peter's churchyard and along Church Street into Titchfield square. This thriving

Beach views at Hill Head

village offers a choice of pubs and several shops, as well as the **Hallmark coffee shop** in South Street.

Cross the square and continue for 130 yds along West Street, then turn left down the lane beside Guessen's Cottage. Cross Gainsborough Mews and keep ahead along the narrow footpath, following it beside a high brick wall to reach Coach Hill. Zigzag right and left into Lower Bellfield and walk as far as the T-junction. Keep ahead here down a narrow path between fences and cross a garage courtyard. Now duck under the barrier and follow the waymarked footpath half-right across a grassy field to meet Posbrook Lane at a stile Ⓓ.

Cross over, turn left and follow the roadside verge for 130 yds before turning right onto the signposted footpath that follows the lane to Great Posbrook Farm. Keep ahead through the kissing-gate and continue to a three-way signpost; fork left, go through the kissing-gate, then turn immediately right along the permissive footpath beside the hedge on your right. Continue to the kissing-gate on Brownwich Lane Ⓔ.

Turn left through the gate and follow the farm track all the way past the houses at Little Brownwich, where the track becomes a concrete road, to a turning on your left Ⓕ.

Ignore this turning and keep ahead along the road as it winds its way to Lower Brownwich Farm. Now fork left through the metal field gate and follow the waymarked track beside the hedge on your right until it sweeps off to the left as the drive to Sea House Ⓖ.

Keep ahead down the narrow path to reach the beach, where there are fine views to the Isle of Wight. From here back to the car park your route follows part of the 60-mile Solent Way that links Milford on Sea with Emsworth Harbour, and the path is waymarked with a seabird on a green arrow. Turn left along the coastal path and follow it up onto the low cliff. Pass a stile and permissive footpath on your left and keep ahead along the coastal path all the way past Cliff Cottage to the chalets at Meon Shore. Zigzag left and right here and walk behind the chalets to rejoin the coast road near Ⓐ.

Now, simply retrace your steps along the sea wall back to the car park at Hill Head. ●

Test Valley rails and trails

Start	Test Way car park at Horsebridge opposite the John o'Gaunt pub
Distance	6½ miles (10.5km)
Height gain	330 feet (100m)
Approximate time	3 hours
Parking	At the start
Route terrain	Old railway line, country tracks and minor roads. Expect some mud in wet weather
Dog friendly	Dogs must be led near farm animals
Ordnance Survey maps	Landranger 185 (Winchester & Basingstoke), Explorer 131 (Romsey, Andover & Test Valley)

GPS waypoints

Start	SU 344 304
A	SU 350 315
B	SU 339 316
C	SU 317 325
D	SU 316 321
E	SU 318 311
F	SU 321 303
G	SU 334 306
H	SU 342 302

The route at first follows a disused railway line and part of the Test Way. Never far from the Test, it then crosses the river in a number of places, providing views of huge silver-flecked trout for which this chalk river is so famous. It turns onto part of the 24-mile- (39km) long Clarendon Way and continues through Houghton village and across farmland. An ancient track crosses the route of an old Roman road, and the path leads back across the river.

Go back to the car park entrance opposite the **John o'Gaunt** pub and turn left onto the road. Pass Horsebridge Mill on the right and, 50 yds beyond the river bridge, turn right onto the Test Way towards Inkpen Beacon. The track follows an old railway line, and soon crosses the river. Continue as far as the gates where the Clarendon Way crosses the old line A.

Turn left onto the Clarendon Way, a long-distance route from Winchester to Salisbury, which crosses carriers of the river a number of times and eventually reaches a tarmac road at Houghton village. If you wish you can turn right here for an 800-yd diversion to the **Boot Inn**. Otherwise, turn left onto the road and continue as far as the junction with

John O'Gaunt, Horsebridge

Horsebridge Mill stands beside the River Test

Faithfulls Drove at Lavender Cottage **B**.

Turn right here, following the waymarked Clarendon Way up the side road, which soon becomes a farm track. Continue all the way past Hayter's Copse and down the hill to a flight of steps.

At the foot of the steps **C** the Clarendon Way turns off to the right past a Millennium Statue by Zoë Whittier. Leave the long-distance route here and turn left onto the drove road, following the waymarked Test Valley Tour.

Drove roads are ancient routes once used to drive animals to market. Keep straight ahead past Hayter's Farm until you reach the crossroads **D**, just a few paces beyond the small concrete bridge that bypasses a ford.

Here again you have the option of a 3/4-mile diversion to a choice of pubs in Broughton. The walk itself goes straight over the crossroads and up The Hollow. Tracks or roads named 'Hollow' are often very ancient routes, so called because they have been worn hollow by traffic and rain. This tarmac road passes houses and soon becomes an earth track which goes under a canopy of tree branches. Ignore footpaths to the right and left. On Broughton Hill ahead a Saxon warrior's skeleton, including his blond hair, was uncovered by a ploughman in the 19th century.

When the track splits into three, and a narrow footpath runs straight ahead, turn left and follow the grass track along the field edge. Keep the hedge on your right, and continue through a windbreak of trees until you reach a tarmac road **E**.

Turn left onto the road, which follows the line of the old Roman road from Winchester to Salisbury. After 200 yds turn right down the no through road opposite an ancient burial mound on your right, and drop down past Heywood Farm to a pair of red brick cottages on your right **F**.

Bear left here, then left again through a metal field gate onto a waymarked green lane. The lane continues onto a concrete road through

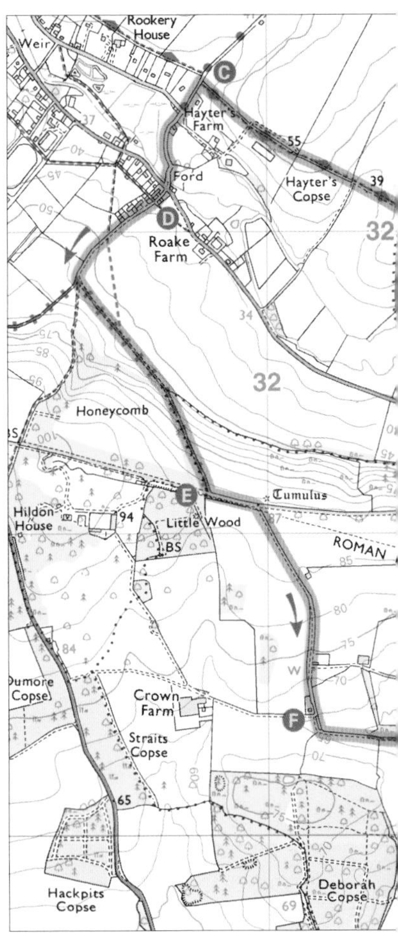

a dairy cattle unit and, beyond the buildings, you follow the bridleway down to a tarmac road. Turn left onto the road and follow it until you reach houses and a farm drive on the left **G**.

Opposite the drive, turn right onto the signposted footpath along a gravel track between fields. On the left is Bossington's tiny country church. A hamlet too once stood here but in 1829 was destroyed by the owner of nearby Bossington House.

A field near here is locally known as 'Agincourt'. In 1415, Henry V, on route with his army for Southampton and the Battle of Agincourt, encamped here, unable to cross the Channel because of unfavourable winds.

Go across the bridge over the river. Look to the left where an old thatched fishing hut creates a delightful picture. Then, after crossing a second bridge over the river, cross the waymarked stile and bear left across a field towards old willow trees. Here a stile leads onto the disused railway line **H**.

Turn left and follow the track, which leads beside the restored Horsebridge station with its signal box and an old carriage standing at the platform. Take the narrow track to the right at the end of the station which leads back into the car park. ●

0 200 400 600 800 METRES 1 KILOMETRES
0 200 400 600 YARDS ½ MILES

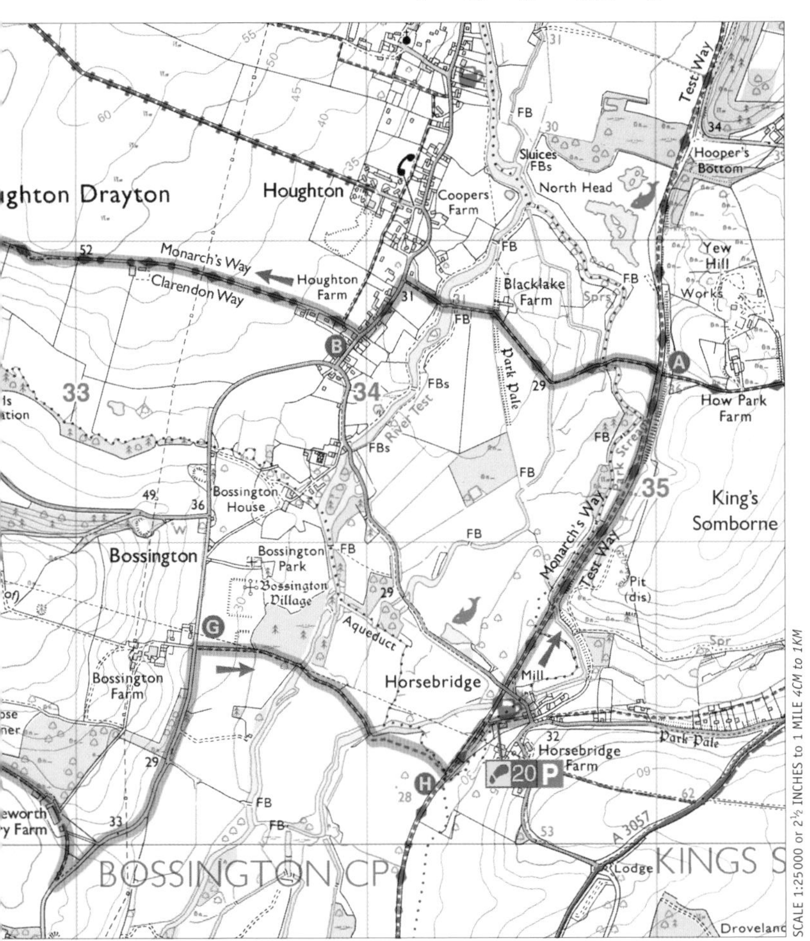

Itchen Abbas & the water babies

Start	Micheldever Wood car park, one mile east of the A33 between Winchester and Basingstoke
Distance	6½ miles (10.5km)
Height gain	490 feet (150m)
Approximate time	3 hours
Parking	At the start
Route terrain	Well-made country tracks and minor roads
Dog friendly	Dogs must be led along public roads, especially the B3047 at Itchen Abbas
Ordnance Survey maps	Landranger 185 (Winchester & Basingstoke), Explorer 132 (Winchester, New Alresford & East Meon)

GPS waypoints

- SU 529 362
- Ⓐ SU 536 357
- Ⓑ SU 555 343
- Ⓒ SU 544 330
- Ⓓ SU 535 331
- Ⓔ SU 540 335
- Ⓕ SU 537 356

In the summer of 1862, Charles Kingsley settled in the Itchen Valley to complete the manuscript of The Water Babies. *Starting from an attractive bluebell wood, this walk climbs over the high chalk downs before dropping into the valley to pass the pub where Kingsley wrote much of his classic fable. The route also passes the forgotten site of an early cricket ground, and crosses the disused tracks of the Mid-Hants Railway.*

In late April and early May, the sight and scent of Micheldever Wood is one of Hampshire's glories, as a thick covering of bluebells carpets the woodland floor. But these colourful woods are soon left behind, and in summer the continuous liquid song of the skylark dominates the wide skies above the upland chalk. Towards the close of the 18th century, before ploughing broke the close-cropped downland turf to create today's arable landscape, the cricketers of Hambledon took on the best of their contemporaries on the downs above Itchen Abbas. Nothing but memory now marks the site of those early games, and for something more substantial we must look to other pioneers.

Halfway round the walk, spare a thought for the sad remains of the Mid-Hants Railway. Originally projected as a local link between Alton and Winchester, the ambitious promoters constructed all their earthworks and bridges for double track. Before the line was finished the company was contemplating plans for a connection with Portsmouth, yet the proposed line was never built and their little railway opened in 1865 with just a single line. It was never to earn its double track.

Turn left out of the car park and follow the road for about 200 yds, then

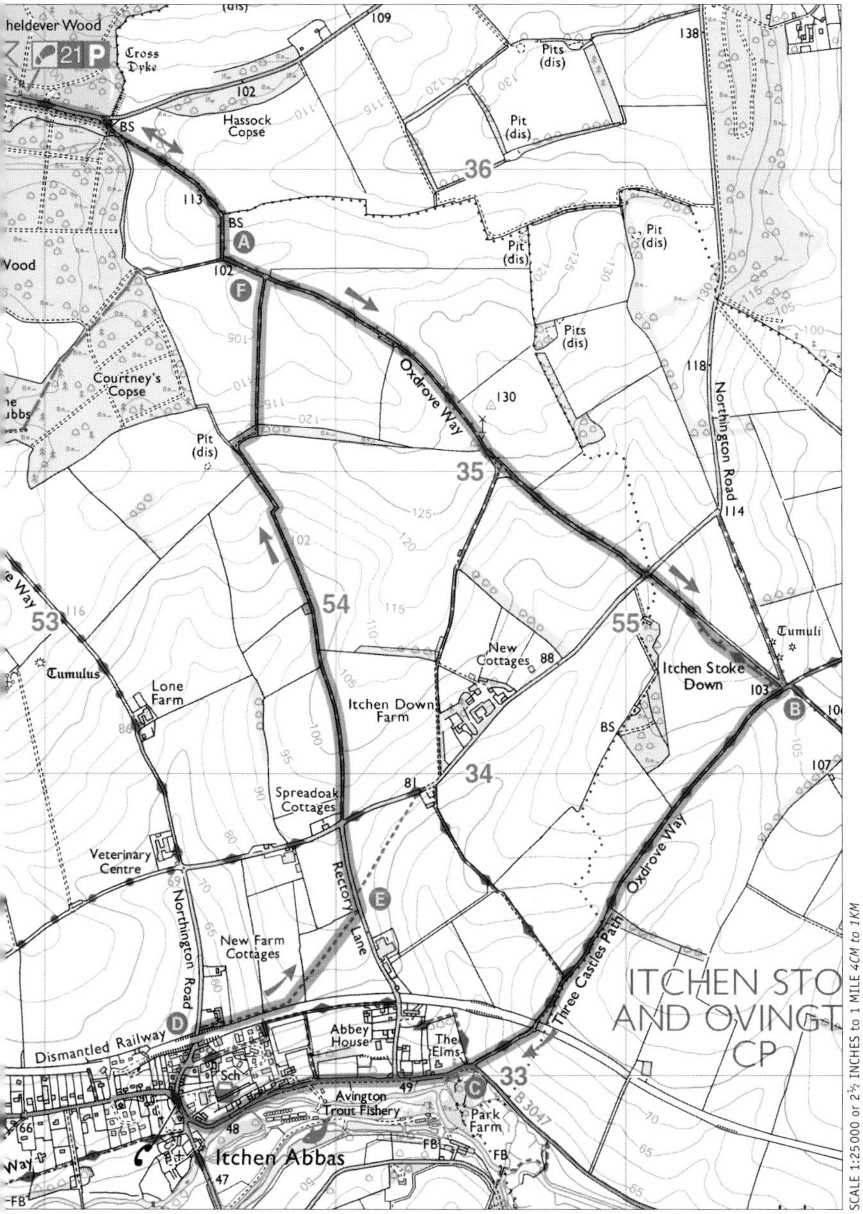

SCALE 1:25 000 or 2½ INCHES to 1 MILE 4CM to 1KM

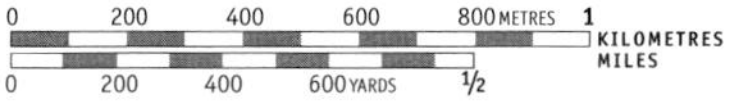

fork right under a metal height barrier onto the waymarked off-road cycle trail. The trail soon leaves the woods, and from here you may glimpse deer grazing in the fields bordering Itchen Wood. Now the path climbs through a tunnel of trees, bears to the right, and drops gently downhill to a fork Ⓐ.

Turn left, and keep ahead past the

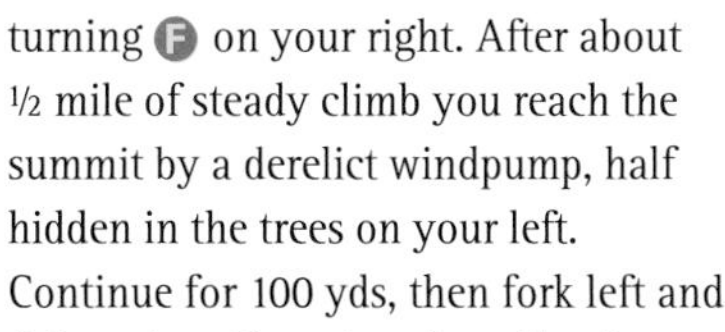

turning Ⓕ on your right. After about ½ mile of steady climb you reach the summit by a derelict windpump, half hidden in the trees on your left. Continue for 100 yds, then fork left and follow the off-road cycle trail as it drops to a crossways with Northington Road. Keep ahead here, following the path as it climbs gently between wire fences onto Itchen Stoke Down.

As early as 1772 the men of Hambledon Old Club were playing cricket at county level. Their first recorded match here on Stoke Down was against England in July 1778. The Hambledon team lost, but the following year England came back to Stoke Down and was beaten in the return match.

The five-way junction on Itchen Stoke Down **B** will try to lead you astray. Ignore the path that trails in from your left, and turn 90 degrees to your right onto a pleasant, grassy path between hedges of hawthorn and dog rose. A short mile farther on, cross the silent tracks of the Mid-Hants Railway, bear right, and drop smartly down to the B3047 **C**.

Turn right along the road, taking great care on this stretch as there's no pavement for most of the way into Itchen Abbas. Here the **Trout Inn** – formerly the Plough – still offers welcome hospitality, just as it did in Charles Kingsley's time. Many of Tom's underwater adventures almost certainly took place in the Itchen, where Kingsley made the most of the peace and quiet for a few days fishing. Continue for 100 yds past The Trout, then turn right up the back lane towards the school and the old railway bridge **D**.

Just beyond the bridge, turn right beside the wooden gate into a farmyard. Keeping the timber buildings on your left, pass through a gateway and over the stile just beyond it. Continue climbing slowly to a gap between two fields, turn half-left, and cross two fields on the same heading. In the far corner of the second field, a gap leads you out onto Rectory Lane **E**.

Turn left up the lane and keep ahead onto the hedged green lane when you reach the crossways at Spreadoak Cottages. The lane climbs steadily for about 1/2 mile, and it's worth stopping regularly to admire the unrivalled views of the Itchen Valley opening up behind you. After winding through a couple of double bends the lane bypasses a metal gate, then drops gently beside a wire fence on your right. A second gate heralds the T-junction where you rejoin your outward route **F**.

Turn left, then right, and retrace the last 1/2 mile to your starting point in the car park. ●

Bluebell wood

Rockbourne and Breamore

Start	Rockbourne
Distance	7 miles (11.3km)
Height gain	690 feet (210m)
Approximate time	3½ hours
Parking	Rockbourne church hall car park
Route terrain	Minor roads, field paths and woodland tracks that will be muddy in the wet
Dog friendly	Please lead dogs near farm animals and shoots, especially from the start to beyond Whitsbury stables; through Breamore Wood; and in Kiln Wood
Ordnance Survey maps	Landranger 184 (Salisbury & The Plain), Explorers OL22 (New Forest) and 130 (Salisbury & Stonehenge)

GPS waypoints

Start	SU 113 182
A	SU 115 184
B	SU 125 195
C	SU 140 205
D	SU 152 185
E	SU 146 177
F	SU 128 171
G	SU 116 179

This attractive route crosses a varied landscape of woodland and rolling farmland to link the pretty village of Rockbourne with the magnificent Elizabethan manor house at Breamore. The walk passes the well-known stud and racing stables on the edge of Whitsbury village, as well as Breamore's ancient miz-maze, a circular labyrinth traditionally used as a penance by monks. With plenty to see at both Rockbourne and Breamore, the walk provides the framework for a full day out, but do check the websites for seasonal opening hours if you intend to visit either of these attractions.

Rockbourne takes its name from the winterbourne or seasonal chalk stream that runs beside the village road. It takes its character too, for residents of the thatched cottages and flint houses clustered beyond the stream must reach the road over numerous little footbridges. The welcoming 16th-century **Rose and Thistle** pub is a joy with its whitewash, thatch and flagstone floors, but the village is mainly famous for its large, 40-room Roman villa. Rediscovered in 1942, the villa stood at the centre of a large farming estate that was occupied for some 350 years. You can walk around the remains of the villa and view some of the fascinating finds in the site museum – for full details, check www.hants.gov.uk/museum/rockbourne

Approaching through the woods, Breamore House comes as something of a surprise. Standing above the Avon Valley, the building has changed little since it was completed in 1583 and the period atmosphere is popular with filmmakers. For visitor information go to www.breamorehouse.com.

Start: Turn left out of the car park and, after 50 yds, turn right up the lane towards Manor Farm. *(Alternatively, keep straight on along the village road to visit the* **Rose and Thistle.***)* Pass the turning to St Andrew's Church on your right, and continue until the bridleway forks at a two-way signpost Ⓐ.

Keep left here, following the grassy track through a gate and up the hill. Continue up the valley past a bridleway signpost and through two metal field gates. After a few paces, a smaller gate leads you onto a charming path that climbs gently through an avenue of old beech trees to a wooden wicket gate. Keep ahead here, go through a further gate, and walk through the more formal beech avenue that leads to the road just beyond Whitsbury Stud. Turn right, and continue for 80 yds.

Turn left onto the signposted bridleway Ⓑ beside the training stables, which has produced some well-known racehorses including Red Rum. Keep right at the corner of the stables, then bear left at the bridleway sign just beyond the buildings. Keep ahead when the track veers off to the left beside a metal gate, where you can glimpse the banks of the hill fort through the trees on your right.

Drop down into the valley bottom to the junction with Long Steeple Lane, then zigzag right and left over a stile and follow the footpath along the right-hand field edge. Keep ahead onto an enclosed green lane at the corner of the field, and carry on up the hill past a corrugated iron barn on your left. Walk through the woodland and continue beside the right-hand field edge to a stile at the brow of the hill Ⓒ.

Cross the stile and turn right onto the waymarked bridleway. After 100 yds, you have the option to fork right and visit the miz-maze, rejoining the bridleway along South Charford Drove a little farther on. Follow the bridleway as it veers right, then left, and drops down through Breamore Wood to emerge beside Breamore House. Keep ahead down the winding gravel drive to a crossways by the ornamental gateposts, where you have the further option of turning right to visit the Saxon church, seasonal museum and **tea barn**. Otherwise, simply keep ahead to reach a lane Ⓓ.

Turn right and follow the lane around the left-hand bend, keeping ahead at

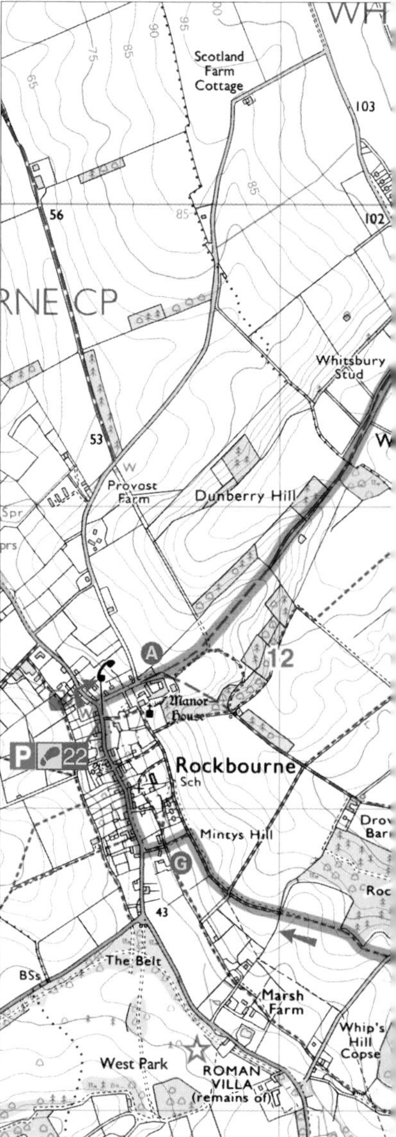

the staggered crossroads towards Whitsbury. Pass Topp's Farm House on your left, and keep ahead briefly at the crossroads towards Fordingbridge until the lane bends sharp left **E**.

Keep straight on along the signposted footpath. This shady track climbs gently past a lone cottage, crosses a stile, and bears left into Kiln Wood. Continue for 100 yds, then fork right off the track at a stout waymark post to join a woodland path. Yellow paint blotches on the trees punctuate your progress until you leave the woods at a waymarked wooden barrier. Keep ahead here, walking parallel with the woods on your right, until you re-enter woodland at a waymark post.

Continue past a silted-up pond on

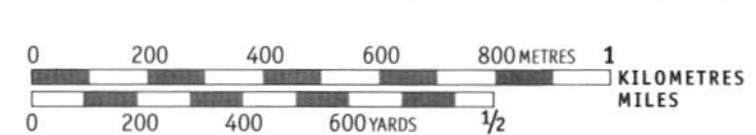

SCALE 1:25 000 or 2½ INCHES to 1 MILE *4CM to 1KM*

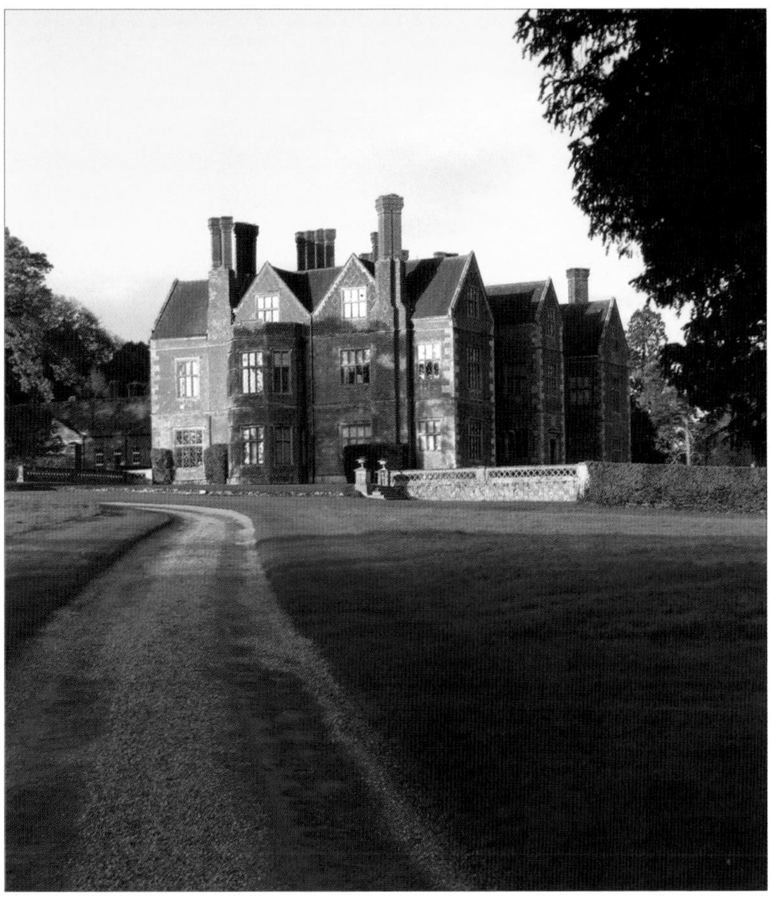

Breamore House

your left and follow the waymarked path through the woods to a junction with a public bridleway. Turn left here, and follow the bridleway until it meets a road at Brookheath House. Turn right for a few paces, then take the signposted footpath on your left and follow it just inside the woodland edge to a T-junction with a gravelled track **F**.

Turn right along the track, pass a turning on your right as you re-enter the woods, then continue to a gate and a tarmac lane. Turn left down the hill for 175 yds to a stile in the hedge on your right. In order to visit the remains of the Roman villa continue down the lane to a T-junction and turn right. Otherwise nip across, and bear half-left across the field to the corner of the woods ahead. Briefly follow the woodland edge, before striking out across a larger field towards the left-hand end of the trees on the far side of the field. Keep ahead beside the signpost onto the enclosed path that runs along the bank between two fields. Keep ahead as two stiles carry the path across a farm track, then continue to a further stile **G**.

Do not cross the stile, but instead turn left through a small metal gate. Now follow the right-hand field edge and continue across a stile that leads you down a short path to the village road. Turn right into the village to return to the church hall car park. ●

Coasting around Keyhaven

		GPS waypoints
Start	The Gun Inn, Keyhaven	SZ 306 914
Distance	Pennington loop: $5\frac{1}{4}$ miles (8.5km) / Hurst Beach 2 miles (3.3km) each way	Ⓐ SZ 308 916 Ⓑ SZ 311 931 Ⓒ SZ 317 935
Height gain	n/a	Ⓓ SZ 322 936
Approximate time	4 hours	Ⓔ SZ 327 933
Parking	Keyhaven Pay and Display car park, opposite the pub. Limited free roadside parking nearby (4 hours maximum stay)	Ⓕ SZ 299 908 Ⓖ SZ 317 898
Route terrain	Country tracks and exposed sea wall paths, with an optional ferry crossing – check www.hurstcastle.co.uk for timings, fares and castle opening hours	
Dog friendly	Dogs must be led near farm animals	
Ordnance Survey maps	Landranger 196 (The Solent & Isle of Wight), Explorer OL22 (New Forest)	

With its coast and country, world class bird watching and stunning views of the Isle of Wight – not to mention a Tudor castle, two pubs, a café and optional ferry trip, this route can justly claim to have it all. It's a flexible walk, too, with two distinct sections that both start and finish at Keyhaven. You can do the whole route in a single day, or complete the Pennington loop in an afternoon and save Hurst Beach for another day. What's more, the little Hurst Castle ferry is a firm favourite with children.

Looking towards Hurst Castle

Pennington Marshes nature reserve is internationally important for the large numbers of seabirds – including common terns, black-headed gulls and oystercatchers – that breed and feed here. In winter thousands of Brent geese visit the marshes. The large creeks penetrating the salt marsh provide them with fish, and at low water wading birds like dunlin and grey plover feed on the exposed mud. Besides the bird life, look out for interesting plants such as glasswort, sea campion and golden samphire.

Pennington loop

Turn right out of the car park, then right again up the no through road beside the harbour. This attractive spot offers good views to Hurst Castle and the Isle of Wight and, just beyond the bridge, the Solent Way swings off along the sea wall on your right A.

Keep straight on, dodge around the five-bar gate across the lane, and pass the nature reserve on the right. Now fork left, squeezing past a large metal gate onto the signposted footpath, and follow the unmade Iley Lane through the attractively restored landscape of former gravel pits. The lane straightens out and heads north for an easy 3/4 mile. At length a farm track turns off to the left, and after 70 yds you'll come to a signpost and gate at the entrance to Efford recycling centre B.

Cross the access road, and continue through a gate onto the sign-posted footpath opposite. Soon the path goes through a metal gate, and you continue along a tarred lane shaded by tall hedges and young oaks until the track ends at a second metal gate. Slip past it, and turn left onto a country lane.

After 150 yds, turn off over a signposted stile on your right C, and follow the footpath along the right-hand field edge. Continue through a gap in the hedge and along the edge of a second field. The path is soon enclosed by a fence on your left; 100 yds farther on, dodge right and left over a stile and keep walking in the same direction,

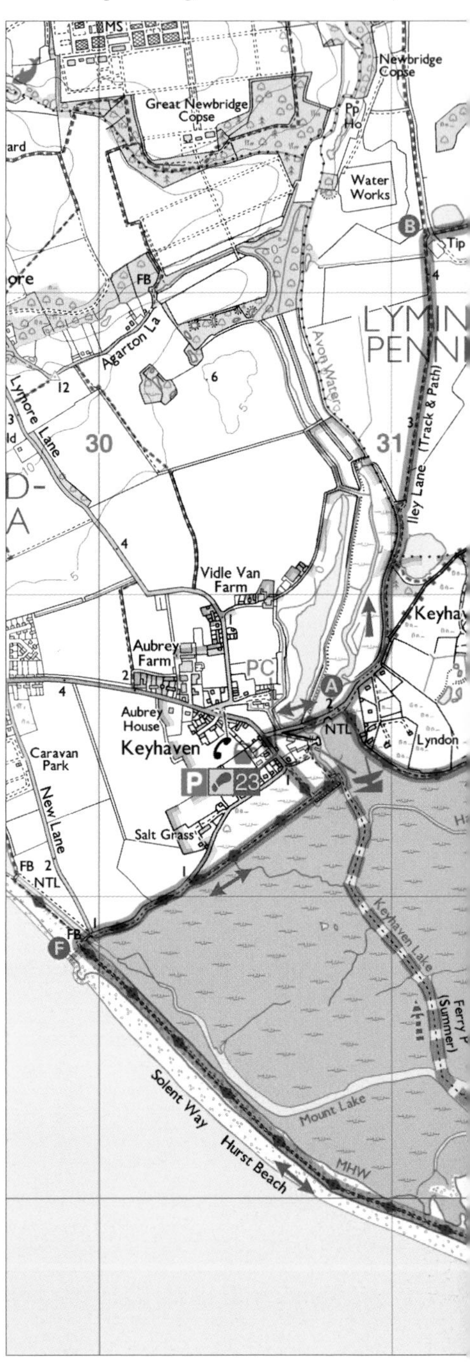

crossing two more stiles before the path ends at Chequers Green. Continue along the drive beside the cottages to join the village road at a letterbox **D**.

Just on your left, **The Chequers** makes a welcome break. To continue the walk, turn right along the lane; then, a few paces beyond the drive to Creek Cottage, turn left onto the enclosed gravel path running parallel with the cottage drive. Bear right after 100 yds, just as you reach a former salt dock, and join the waymarked Solent Way along the bank of the dock with the water on your left. Turn left through a wicket gate **E**, then up the steps beside the sluice and keep ahead along the sea wall path.

From here, route finding is as simple as following the sea wall back to Keyhaven, freeing you to admire the wildlife and breathtaking views. Hurst Castle stands out clearly in the foreground, and flotillas of small sailing craft plough the Solent in a constantly changing panorama that stretches from Newtown to the Needles.

On the landward side, large numbers of seabirds feed around the fringes of shallow

0 200 400 600 800 METRES 1 KILOMETRES
0 200 400 600 YARDS ½ MILES

lagoons – sad reminders of the salt pans that were a mainstay of the local economy for 700 years. At the start of the 19th century the Lymington area produced 6,000 tons annually, valued at a shilling (5p) a bushel. Salt was already highly taxed, but a new levy of 15 shillings (75p) a bushel was imposed to help finance the Napoleonic wars and, by 1845, the local industry had collapsed.

At length, the sea wall sweeps right towards Keyhaven and meets the road. Turn left through the pedestrian gate Ⓐ, then retrace your outward route over the bridge and back to your car.

Hurst Beach

Turn left out of the car park, following the brown signs to Hurst Castle. After 40 yds, keep ahead down the gravelled path as Saltgrass Lane turns off to the right. Turn right at the T-junction and follow the Solent Way along the sea wall, then rejoin Saltgrass Lane at the kissing-gate and bear left along the roadside path until the lane bends away to the right.

Cross a wooden footbridge Ⓕ, bear left up the slope onto Hurst Beach, and follow the track to Hurst Castle. Keep left as you approach the castle buildings and follow the path around to the castle entrance and ferry quay Ⓖ.

The castle, completed in 1544, was one of a chain of forts built by Henry VIII 'with all speed, and without sparing any cost'. Following his split with Rome and the dissolution of the monasteries, the king feared an invasion by European Catholics – that invasion never came, but the line of forts stretching from Falmouth to Deal remains a testament to Henry's insecurity.

Hurst Castle was modernised in the Victorian era, and equipped with search-lights and gun batteries for service in the Second World War. Now open to the public, the castle's attractions include the Trinity House lighthouse exhibition, ENSA's Garrison Theatre, and a small **café** in the castle grounds.

After your visit, simply retrace your steps to Keyhaven. Or, for a different view of this fascinating area, treat yourself to a ferry ride back to the start.

The Solent Way

Meon Valley rails and trails

		GPS waypoints
Start	Beaconhill Beeches, 1½ miles north-west of Meonstoke	SU 598 227
Distance	7¾ miles (12.5km)	Ⓐ SU 602 221
Height gain	720 feet (220m)	Ⓑ SU 617 205
Approximate time	4 hours	Ⓒ SU 628 218
Parking	Beacon Hill Natural England car park	Ⓓ SU 641 235
		Ⓔ SU 626 236
		Ⓕ SU 612 233
Route terrain	Paths across farmland, country lanes, and a long stretch of the Meon Valley railway trail. Expect some mud in wet weather	
Dog friendly	Dogs must be led near farm animals, especially at Wheely Down Farm	
Ordnance Survey maps	Landranger 185 (Winchester & Basingstoke), Explorer 119 (Meon Valley, Portsmouth, Gosport & Fareham)	

Starting close to the summit of Beacon Hill in the South Downs National Park, the walk begins with commanding views over the Meon Valley as it joins the South Downs Way and drops into the pretty village of Exton. Here it crosses the river and follows the Meon Valley railway trail for an easy couple of miles into West Meon, where you'll find pubs and an internet café. The route heads back through farmland to rejoin the South Downs Way for the climb back to the finish at Beacon Hill.

Although the walk bypasses Beacon Hill National Nature Reserve, you can take the signposted track for a short diversion into this important area of flower-rich chalk grassland.

About a third of the route follows the impressive earthworks of the Meon Valley railway trail. The line was one of many secondary routes built by the private railway companies in the early 20th century to defend their territories. In this bid to stop the Great Western from reaching the south coast ports, the Waterloo-based London & South Western sank over half a million pounds in a commercial disaster. Their line was built for speed, with lavish stations and earthworks laid out for double track. Yet it opened in 1903 with a single line of rails, and the traffic never justified a second track.

With your back to the road, set off along the public footpath that leaves the car park through a gap just to the right of the South Downs Way bridleway track. Follow the signposted heading across the field towards a small clump of young fir trees, then climb the stile in the far hedge and turn left onto the road. Continue 400 yds to a signposted stile on your left Ⓐ.

Turn left over the stile, then bear gently right, dropping away from the right-hand hedge towards a waymarked stile. Clip the corner of the next field, cross two more stiles and continue over the series of stiles that leads you diagonally through the next five fields to a substantial 'South Downs Way walkers' signpost. Keep ahead here through the gap, then bear left along the left-hand hedge and continue through a kissing-gate to meet Church Lane.

Turn right, then left at the T-junction, and walk down to the junction with Shoe Lane. Keep ahead here, cross the river, and stop at the A32. Take care as you cross this busy main road into Stocks Lane, and keep ahead past Rectory Lane until you reach the junction with Shavards Lane B.

Turn right here, go under the broken railway bridge, then turn immediately left up the slope to join the former railway line. Cross the South Downs Way at Garden Hill Lane and carry on for half a mile until you reach the slope down to Peake New Road C.

Cross over by the missing bridge, keep ahead up the slope, and continue walking along the old railway. The line dives into a cutting as you approach Hayden Farm, where Old Winchester Hill Lane soars overhead on a massive masonry arch. The line escapes briefly from the cutting to steal across the track from Brocklands Farm before entering the site of West Meon station D.

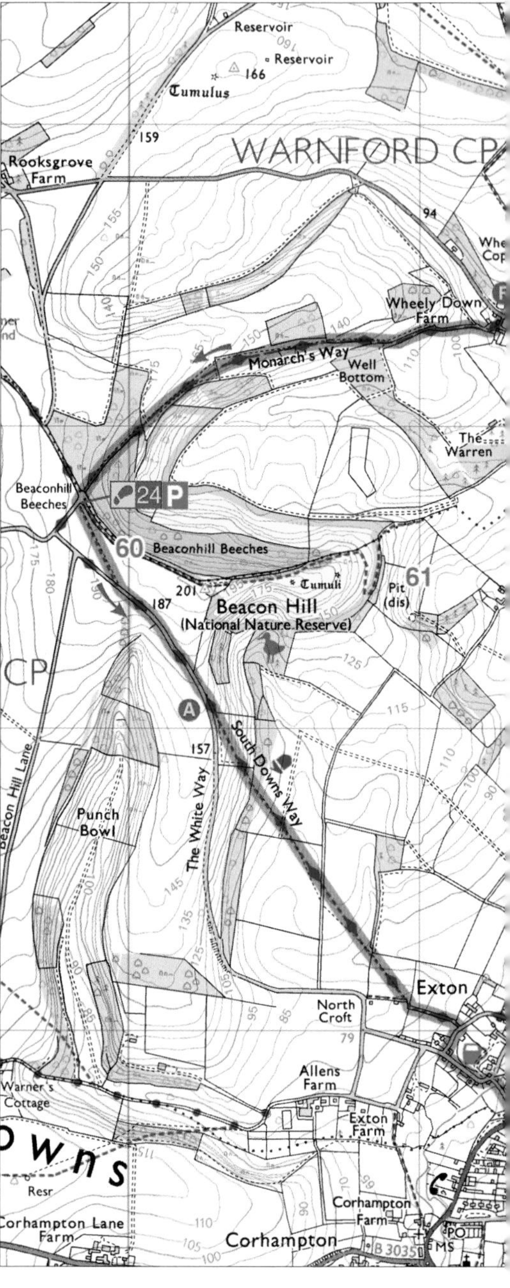

Fork right here to explore the old platforms and the towering embankment that once carried trains onto the 62-feet high steel viaduct that was demolished soon after the line was closed. Otherwise, walk through the parking area and fork left down the old station approach towards West Meon.

SCALE 1:25 000 or 2½ INCHES to 1 MILE *4CM to 1KM*

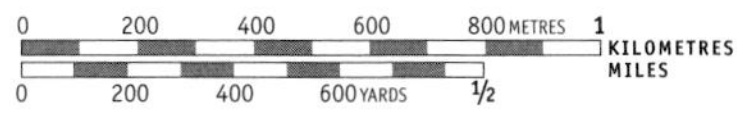

Turn left at the junction with Station Road and drop down to the village and A32. You can turn right here for a break at the **Red Lion** or the **Thomas Lord** pubs (The latter is named after the founder of Lord's cricket ground, who is buried in the churchyard).

To continue the walk, zigzag left and right across the A32, watching carefully for traffic on this awkward bend. Join the signposted footpath beside

St Peter and Paul Church, Exton

'Warnford Corner' cottage, cross a drive and continue into the churchyard. The church was designed by Sir Gilbert Scott and consecrated in 1846.

Halfway along the gravel path to the church, turn left between the gravestones to a stone-built stile in the churchyard wall. Nip across, and follow the enclosed path out past the large converted barn houses and cross the access road into the field ahead. Keep ahead, following the hedge line on your right and keeping parallel with the A32 in the valley on your left. Go through a gap in the hedge at the end of the field, cross a stile, and continue beside the right-hand hedge to a stile leading out onto Lippen Lane near Beaconsfield Farm **E**.

Turn left, and follow this winding lane past the houses and back to the A32. Turn right briefly along the road-side pavement, pass Rose Lea Cottage, and take the next turning right towards **The Milbury's** pub. Pass The Wheel Horse on your left, and continue to the farm entrance just before Wheely Down Forge **F**.

Turn left onto the signposted bridleway (waymarked The Monarch's Way) and bear right past the farm buildings to begin the climb back to Beaconhill Beeches. Soon the signposted bridleway leaves the farm track through a metal gate on your right, turning immediately left to follow the left-hand field edge. Go through the gate at the far corner of this narrowing field and walk along the enclosed bridleway before continuing beside the wire fence on your left for 220 yds.

At the end of the fence the waymarked path bears left along an unfenced grassy track that leads to wooden gates at the entrance to Beaconhill Beeches. Keep ahead through the gate, now following the well-made gravel track that makes light work of the short woodland walk back to your car.

Denmead and the cradle of cricket

		GPS waypoints
Start	Denmead (junction of B2150 and Kidmore Lane)	SU 659 120
Distance	9 miles (14.5km)	Ⓐ SU 654 128
Height gain	720 feet (220m)	Ⓑ SU 655 133
Approximate time	4 hours	Ⓒ SU 646 152
Parking	Kidmore Lane car park	Ⓓ SU 653 162
Route terrain	Field paths and tracks that may be muddy, with short sections of country lane	Ⓔ SU 662 175 Ⓕ SU 668 171 Ⓖ SU 676 166 Ⓗ SU 669 152 Ⓙ SU 664 141
Dog friendly	Dogs must be led near farm animals	
Ordnance Survey maps	Landrangers 196 (The Solent & Isle of Wight) and 185 (Winchester & Basingstoke), Explorer 119 (Meon Valley, Portsmouth, Gosport & Fareham)	

The English summer game had its origins in the high downland north of Denmead where, in the second half of the 18th century, the Bat & Ball pub on Broadhalfpenny Down was the centre of the cricketing world. This enjoyable route weaves together sections from two long-distance paths on a cross-country pilgrimage to this isolated hostelry, where you can still stroll across the road to watch the cricket on a summer's afternoon. Check www.broadhalfpennydown.com for the fixtures list before you set out.

For almost 30 years, the Hambledon Club played cricket opposite the Bat & Ball. This was no mere coincidence, for the team's captain, Richard Nyren, was also the pub's landlord. Throughout this time the Hambledon Club played – and defeated – the best of the rest of England, reaching its climax in 1775 when Nyren contributed 98 runs to help defeat Surrey with a second innings score of 357. This was the golden age of the Hambledon Club, which established and refined the laws of cricket. By 1780 the Club had moved to a less exposed ground nearer the village and, with the formation of the MCC in 1787, the initiative passed from Hampshire to London.

Yet Broadhalfpenny Down was not dead, but merely sleeping. Cricket matches resumed here after 1908 at the instigation of the legendary C B Fry, and Winchester College bought the freehold in 1920. The modern history of the ground was secured in 1958, when officers from the nearby Royal Naval Signals School at HMS Mercury founded the Broadhalfpenny Brigands

Cricket Club to restore regular cricket to this historic ground.

Leave the car park by the vehicle exit and turn right into Kidmore Lane. After 200 yds turn left at Broad View Cottage onto the signposted Cemetery Lane footpath, and keep ahead when the tarmac ends at the burial ground. At the far corner of the burial ground, turn right onto the signposted Wayfarers' Walk and follow the path as it winds over a plank bridge and up the right-hand side of an open field.

Cross the waymarked stile Ⓐ in the corner of the field, and keep ahead along the right-hand edge of the next field until the hedge bears away to your left.

Just here, nip over the stile on your right Ⓑ, turn left onto the lane, then right at the junction 50 yds farther on. Continue for 70 yds, then follow the signposted Wayfarers' Walk (WW) as it strikes off on a cross-field path to your left. Pass through the hedge near an electricity post and turn left along the edge of the next field to reach Rushmere Lane. Turn right for 100 yds, then left at

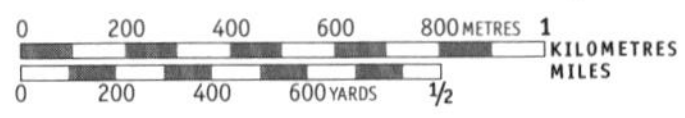

a WW waymark post along the right-hand field edge. Now follow the WW waymarks through a gap in the hedge, and continue along the right-hand edge of the next field. Go through a gap at the top corner of the next field and keep ahead along the edge of the field, following the path as it zigzags left, then right, to reach a lane.

Cross the lane and keep ahead, following the WW across the field to a waymarked stile. Nip over, and follow the footpath as it drops steeply through two wooden gates, then bears right to meet Speltham Hill at a kissing-gate. Turn left into the village centre. Just to your left, the village shop offers take-away snacks and hot drinks, while **The Vine** stands a little farther down West Street. To continue the walk, keep ahead at the staggered crossroads, and walk up High Street towards the church. Fork right at the gate, following the 'WW circular' route through the churchyard, then cross Church Lane to the village school Ⓒ.

The Bat & Ball

Chidden
Chidden Farm
Big West End Farm
Grove Copse
Hyden Cottage
Shuttlecock Cottages
Hermitage Farm
Beckless Plantation
Beckless Farm
Beckless Cottages
Beckless Copse
Chidden Holt Farm
Chidden Holt
The Peak
Pit (dis)
Tumuli
Cricket Ground
Mon
Bat and Ball
Park Wood
HAMBLEDON CP
Cricket Ground
Brook Lane
Scotland Farm
Monarch's Way
Windmill Down
Park Farm
Park House
Whitedale Farm
Whitedale House
Dogkennel Lane
Broadhalfpenny Down
The Hangers
Scotland
Glidden Lane
Glidden Farm
Microlight Site
Fairfield House
Hambledon House
PO
Little Hanger
Stud Farm
Ton Wood
Veniss Row
Greasteds Copse
Pitt Hill Lane (Track)
Horsepost Lane
Harrowgate Lane
Rushmere
Rushmere Pond
Rushmere Farm
Veniss Copse
Pits (dis)
Denmead Mill
Sawyer's Hill
Rushmere Lane
Mill Copse
Pithill Farm
Steane Copse
Vinnell's Wood
Millfield Farm
Crabdens Row
El Sub Sta
Broadway Lane
Well Hill
Port Copse Plantation
Pitthill Farm
Rookwood Farm
Stoneacre Copse
Crabdens Copse
Forest Gate
Roman Dell (Pit (disused))
The Crossways
Broadway Farm
Kidmore Lane
Little Denmead Farm
Denmead Farm
High Wood
Alexandra
Anthill Common
Wayfarer's Walk
Pyles Farm
White Horse Lane
Denmead Lane
The Arrows
Eastland Gate
Harts Copse
Tanner's Lane
Cemy
Inhams Farm
Glasspool Farm
Hambledon Rd
Merritt's Farm
Denmead
Shrover
Inhams La
B 2150
PC
Shafters Farm
Anmore Dell
Forest Road
Kings Pond
Clarendon Farm
Anmore
CP Bdy
A
B
C
D
E
F
G
H
J
12
13
14
15
16
17
25
65
66
67

The Hambledon stone

Take the lane to the right of the school, keeping ahead onto a hedged path. Cross a Tarmac drive and continue between the vines of Hambledon vineyard. Leave the vineyard at a stile, turn left, and follow the narrow enclosed path up the hill until it turns right over a stile and heads across a field to a second stile. Cross over, go through the corner of the wood to a further stile, then bear left across the next field to reach Brook Lane Ⓓ.

Keep ahead along the right-hand edge of the Hambledon Cricket Club ground. The successors to the great 18th-century Club now field their own players here on Ridge Meadow, 1½ miles closer to the village. Among their modern achievements was reaching the final of the national village knock-out cup at Lords in 1989, and the club still works hard to offer an extensive and successful coaching programme.

Leave the ground in the far corner and keep ahead across the next field. Continue with woodland on your right-hand side to a gap in the hedge; bear right here along the signposted path across the field, steering just to the right of Hermitage Farm, half hidden in the trees ahead. Cross the stile on the far side of this large field and keep ahead onto the gently curving green lane, soon joining a tarmac drive. Leaving Hermitage Farmhouse on your right, walk up the drive to meet a lane Ⓔ.

Turn right, and follow this quiet country lane as it winds down through a shallow valley.

At the brow of the next hill turn left through a gateway Ⓕ and walk up the left-hand side of the field to a stile. Cross over and turn right, following the 'WW circular' route beside a post and wire fence. Continue over three stiles to reach a road, and turn right to the **Bat & Ball** pub Ⓖ.

Turn right at the crossroads and continue as far as the turning for Chidden. Just here, turn left over the stile and walk up the hill to a second stile, now following the Monarch's Way as it turns right along a gravelled farm track. The track passes through woodland and bends to the left before dropping gently past Scotland Cottage. Leave the track here and fork left along the signposted footpath for 375 yds, until it meets a track Ⓗ.

Turn right here, then keep left at the next junction to reach a fork. Keep left here too and, after a further 250 yds, fork left off the track onto a narrower green lane that meanders down the valley side to a junction in the valley bottom Ⓙ.

Keep ahead, taking the shady green track up the hill and continuing to a crossways with minor roads.

Keep straight on towards Denmead, and follow Tanner's Lane around to the right when White Horse Lane turns off to your left. Continue to the T-junction with Kidmore Lane, then turn left for the short distance back to your car. ●

Bentley and the Hampshire Downs

Start	Bentley Memorial Hall, on crossroads of the main village street and Hole Lane
Distance	9¼ miles (15km)
Height gain	740 feet (225m)
Approximate time	4½ hours
Parking	Car park in Hole Lane, just behind the hall
Route terrain	Muddy field paths and country tracks, with short lengths of minor road
Dog friendly	Dogs must be led near horses and farm animals, especially near Pax Hill and west of Blunden's Farm
Ordnance Survey maps	Landranger 186 (Aldershot & Guildford), Explorer 144 (Basingstoke, Alton & Whitchurch)

GPS waypoints

Start	SU 783 439
A	SU 777 442
B	SU 761 430
C	SU 746 442
D	SU 740 454
E	SU 760 464
F	SU 769 458
G	SU 765 443

Setting out from Bentley at the foot of the Hampshire Downs, this route explores the surprisingly remote countryside between the A31 and the M3. After meandering along the valley past Pax Hill, you climb steadily through a farmed landscape studded with woodlands. An appealing byway leads to the tiny village of Well, where there's the opportunity for a break at The Chequers.

Turn left out of the car park and walk up Hole Lane. Keep ahead when Hole Lane bends off to the right, and continue for a few paces past the junction with Church Lane. Now turn left along the signposted footpath, continuing past the houses and through two gates to follow the left-hand hedge along the side of an open field. Pass through a gap in the hedge and keep ahead to a three-way signpost **A**.

Turn left, then right after 50 yds, and continue through a kissing-gate along a tree-shaded path to a wooden signpost. Turn left here down the drive to Pax Hill; then, after 140 yds, turn right over a signposted stile. Walk briefly beside the left-hand hedge, then keep ahead along the signposted path across the open field. Cross the waymarked causeway straight ahead and keep ahead at the next three-way signpost to follow the gravelled drive in front of Coldrey Farm.

Keep ahead as the drive swings right, go through a waymarked gate and continue to a tarmac road. Turn right along the road; then, immediately before the picturesque **Anchor Inn**, turn left along the signposted footpath to follow the right-hand edge of an open field. Dodge left and right at the end of the field, cross a plank bridge, then turn left through a gap in the hedge.

Continue beside the ditch on your left, following its winding course across the field to meet a lane **B**.

Turn right along the lane, then right again at the T-junction in Upper Froyle. Walk past Blunden's Farm Cottage on your left as far as Rye Bridge, then turn left onto the signposted footpath that leads up a hedged track. Continue beside the left-hand hedge to a four-way signpost, then follow the winding green track through the shallow valley ahead. When the track bends sharp right, bear half right across the field, climbing gently and walking diagonally towards a broken stile before continuing on the same heading across the next field.

Pause near the right-hand corner of the woods at the far side of the field to admire the view behind you, then walk through the gap and across the next field to a three-way signpost **C**.

Bear left onto the wider track, and follow it until it bends away to the left. Keep ahead here, along the signposted path beside the right-hand field edge to a waymark post in the corner of Little Wood. Turn right, skirting the woods on your left as you drop down to cross a green track before climbing again beside woodland on your right. Keep ahead past a waymark post at the corner of the woods, striking out across the field towards the road that borders the conifers ahead. Turn left onto the road, pass a small pond, then fork right towards Long Sutton. Crest the short hill and drop down to the junction at Sutton Common **D**.

Turn right here onto the signposted byway; ignore all turnings and follow this charming track until it meets the lane at Well **E**.

Turn left into the village, just as far as the crossroads and the well that was given to the inhabitants by William Fullerton of Well Manor. If you fancy a break, turn left here for the short diversion to **The Chequers**. To continue the walk, turn right towards Dippenhall and follow the road for ½ mile to the

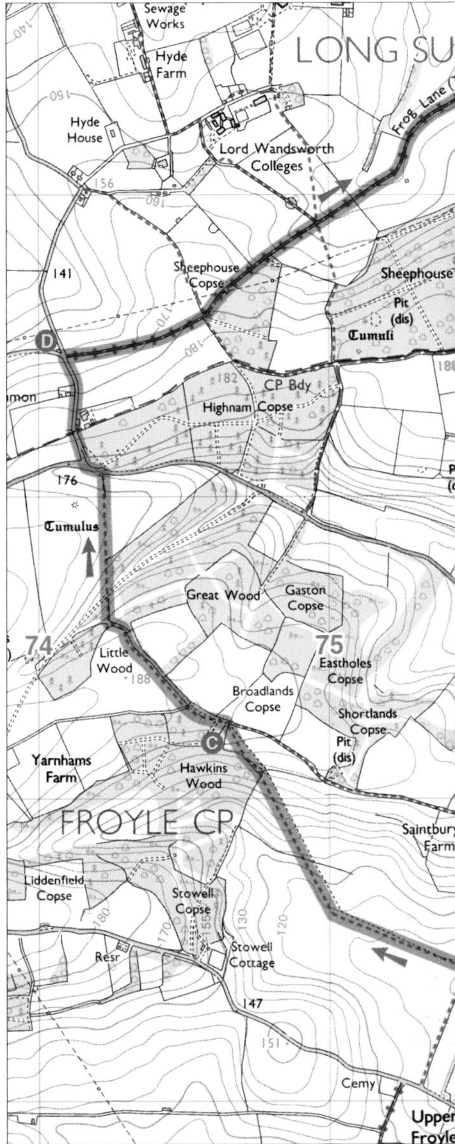

next junction. Turn right, and continue until the road swings sharp left at the foot of the hill F.

Keep ahead here onto the byway and simply follow it until it matures into a metalled lane. Continue to a stile on your left G, about 50 yds past the oast houses on the right. These distinctive buildings with their conical roofs would originally have been used for drying hops or malt, and reflect the long tradition of brewing in the Alton area.

Turn right over the stile and walk diagonally across the field to a stile in the far corner. Cross a second stile a few paces farther on, then turn right to walk beside the hedge on your right to a stile and plank bridge in the corner. Cross over and turn right, then left, to follow the right-hand field edge until it meets a belt of trees at the top of the slope.

Bear right, then left through a gap in the trees, before turning right to continue along the right-hand edge of the next field to a stile. Continue as before, now with the buildings of Pax Hill for company on your right. At the end of the buildings, dodge right through a gap by a waymark post and turn left onto an enclosed path that soon bends right around the edge of the paddocks to rejoin your outward route A.

Turn left here, following the hedge on your right through two fields and two gates, then past the houses to reach a road. Turn right, and keep ahead down Hole Lane to return to your car.

0 200 400 600 800 METRES 1 KILOMETRES

0 200 400 600 YARDS ½ MILES

Stockbridge and Danebury Hill

Start	Stockbridge High Street
Distance	10 miles (16km) / 9¼ miles (14.8km) from Ⓐ
Height gain	310 feet (95m)
Approximate time	4½ hours
Parking	Roadside parking in Stockbridge, or lay-by at point Ⓐ
Route terrain	Country tracks, old railway path and short sections of public roads, some of which are not recommended for children or dogs
Dog friendly	Dogs must be led near farm animals and along public roads
Ordnance Survey maps	Landranger 185 (Winchester & Basingstoke), Explorer 131 (Romsey, Andover & Test Valley)

GPS waypoints

- SU 355 351
- Ⓐ SU 361 358
- Ⓑ SU 359 371
- Ⓒ SU 335 375
- Ⓓ SU 358 391
- Ⓔ SU 374 388
- Ⓕ SU 382 390

Visitors to Stockbridge can hardly fail to notice the imposing Georgian features of the Grosvenor Hotel, with its distinctive porch topped by an overhanging first floor room. Standing halfway along the High Street, the building is home to the exclusive Houghton Club that has regulated fly-fishing on the River Test since 1822. From here, the route passes close to the iconic Danebury Hill Fort before meandering along a delightful dry valley to meet the River Test at Fullerton. An easy riverside stroll along the abandoned 'Sprat and Winkle' railway line completes the circle back to Stockbridge.

The Andover and Redbridge Railway had its origins in an 18th-century canal that had followed much of the same route. Though profitable in its early years, the canal inevitably suffered from the rise of the railways in the mid-19th century, and eventually it fell victim to one of the territorial battles so beloved of the Victorian railway companies.

Backed by the Great Western with its eyes fixed firmly on the south coast, work began to convert the canal to a broad gauge railway in 1859. Lord Palmerston cut the first sod to the sound of a 14-gun salute – yet, despite this optimistic start, the nominally independent Andover and Redbridge Company was bankrupt within two years. The London & South Western Railway eventually completed the work in 1865. Twenty years later, a link line was added between Hurstbourne and Fullerton Junction, where this walk joins the Test Way along the old trackbed.

Head east along Stockbridge High Street to the roundabout opposite the **White Hart**, and bear left to follow the Test Way along the grass verge beside the A30. *This first section of the Test Way is not recommended for children or dogs.* Keep ahead towards Andover at the next roundabout, and continue for 350 yds to a lay-by on your left Ⓐ.

Longstock eel trap

Branch off to the left here, now following the Test Way along the old railway track. Just before the first overbridge, fork left and climb up to meet the back lane to Longstock. Turn left along the lane, looking out for the replica eel traps on your right as you cross the hump-backed bridge over the River Test. During the 1930s, Test Valley eels were sent by train from Fullerton to supply the popular jellied eel trade in London's East End. Continue to the junction at the **Peat Spade** pub in Longstock Ⓑ.

Turn left as far as St Mary's Church, then right up Church Road. Continue past the houses and keep ahead at the end of the tarmac, heading west along the gravelled bridleway. Pass the barns at New Buildings and pause here to look at the panoramic views opening up behind you. At the crest of the hill, the tree-clad slopes of Danebury hill fort heave into view on the horizon directly ahead. Continue to the road at a small parking area just beyond a metal height barrier Ⓒ.

Turn right, and fork immediately left to visit Danebury Hill. This notable Iron Age hill fort was once a thriving settlement, surrounded by its defensive earthworks and wooden palisade. Archaeologists have discovered the remains of thatched roundhouses, as well as storage pits for agricultural produce. Danebury also supported craft industries like metal and leather working, spinning and weaving. Religious ceremonies took place near the highest part of the enclosure, which was abandoned about a century before the Roman invasion of Britain. Unfortunately there are no public rights of way leading to the Danebury site. *You should take extreme care if making the short diversion along this busy road, which is not recommended for children or dogs.*

To continue the main route, take the quieter right-hand fork towards the Clatfords. Follow the road for 400 yds, then turn right onto the waymarked bridleway past the attractive brick and flint buildings of Daisy Down Farm. Half a mile farther on, the gravelled farm track swings away to the right. Keep ahead under a metal barrier, following the waymarked route along a rutted green track. Another track swings in from your left shortly before you pass under some electricity wires, and the bridleway continues to meet a road just beyond a metal height barrier Ⓓ.

Cross over and keep ahead along the signposted bridleway, passing the entrance to Fullerton Down House after a few paces. Now simply follow this attractive winding green lane past the

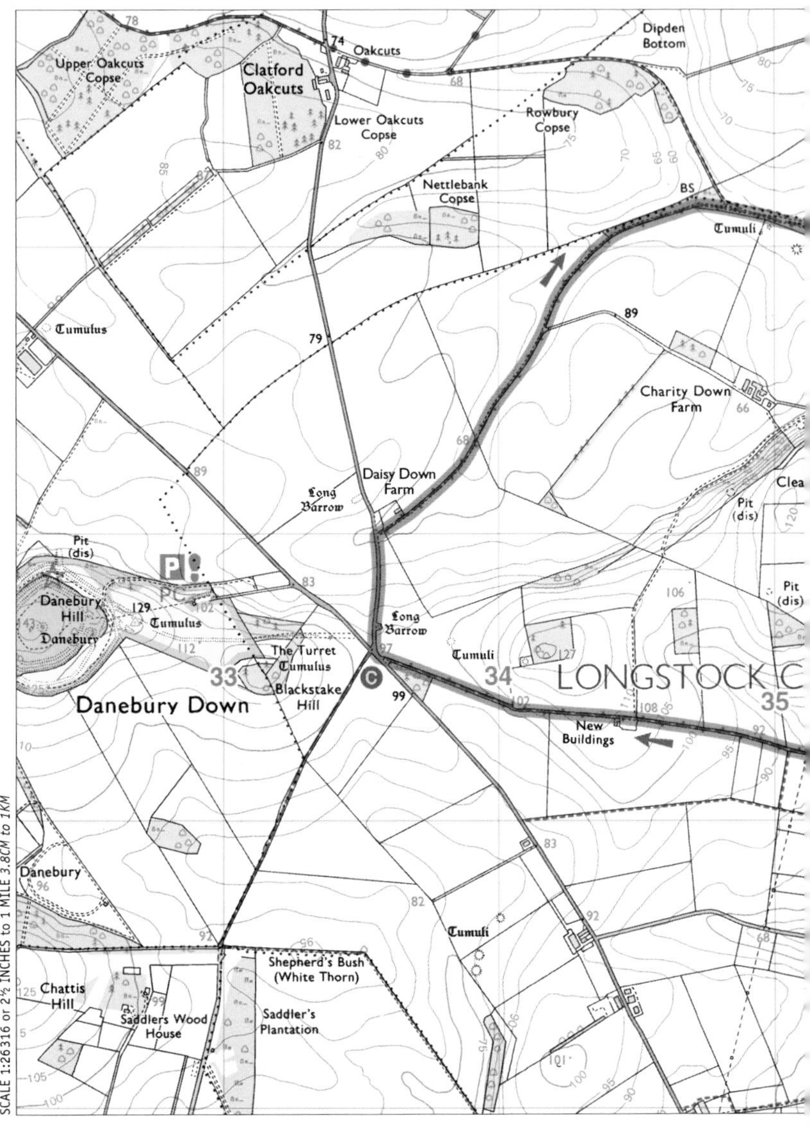

humps and bumps of the medieval field system on your right, until you reach a road **E**.

Turn left along the road, and keep right at the junction towards Wherwell. Cross the bridge at Fullerton Mill and stop at the A3057. *Take extreme care as you cross this busy road, turn left, and continue for 100 yds beyond the old railway bridge.* At the letterbox, turn sharp right onto the permissive bridlepath that leads to the Test Way at the former Fullerton Junction station.

Pass The Old Railway Cottages and keep ahead under the metal barrier to walk along the old station platform, then down the ramp to follow the Test Way along the old railway track. Soon the route lives up to its name, crossing the river on a girder bridge before continuing to a brick arched bridge over the old line **F**.

From here you can make a short diversion to the popular **Mayfly** pub.

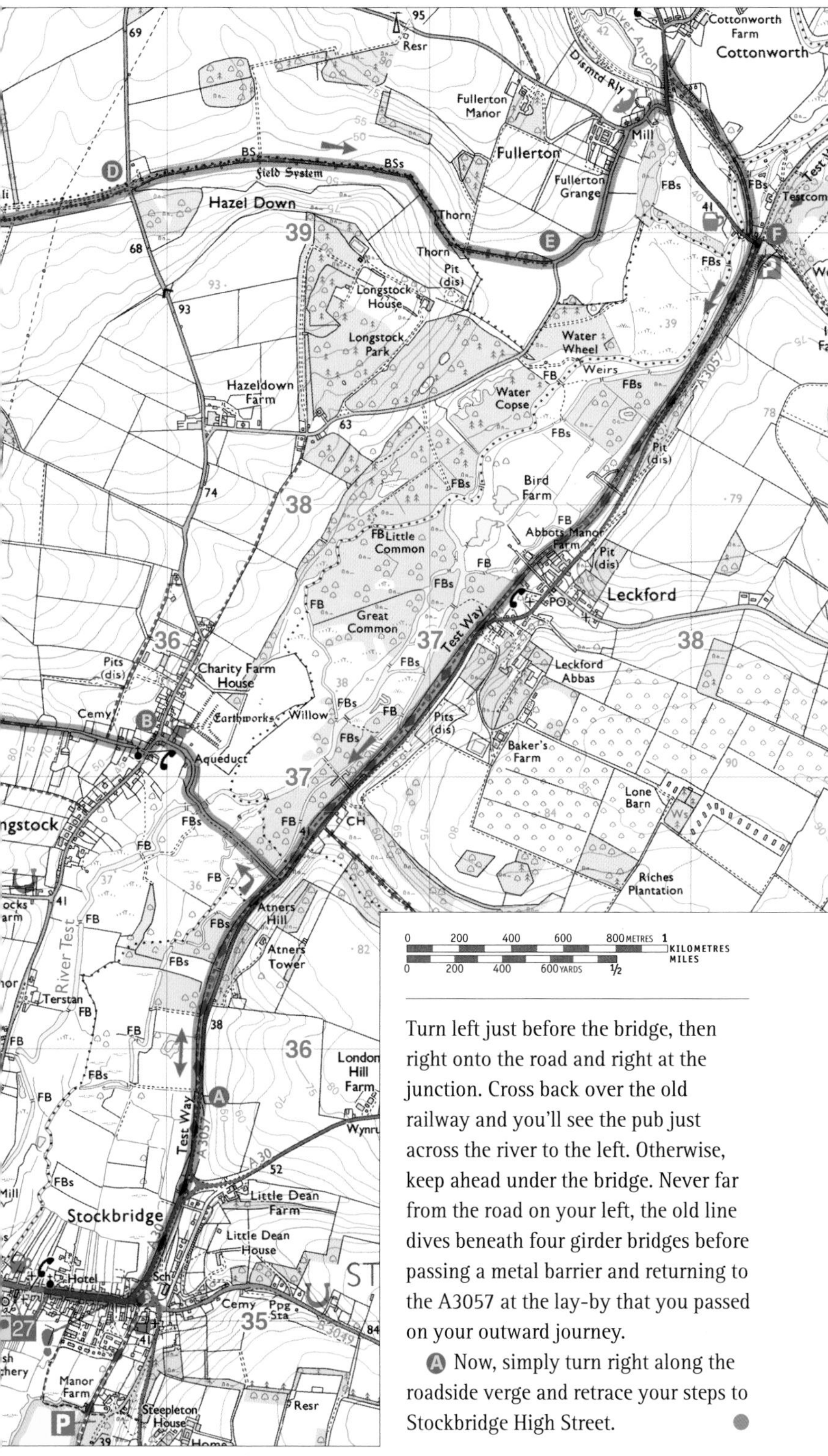

Turn left just before the bridge, then right onto the road and right at the junction. Cross back over the old railway and you'll see the pub just across the river to the left. Otherwise, keep ahead under the bridge. Never far from the road on your left, the old line dives beneath four girder bridges before passing a metal barrier and returning to the A3057 at the lay-by that you passed on your outward journey.

Ⓐ Now, simply turn right along the roadside verge and retrace your steps to Stockbridge High Street.

Kingsclere and Watership Down

Start	Kingsclere, Anchor Road
Distance	10¼ miles (16.5km)
Height gain	935 feet (285m)
Approximate time	5 hours
Parking	Anchor Yard car park in Anchor Road, just off Swan Street
Route terrain	Country tracks and field paths, some of which will be muddy after rain
Dog friendly	Dogs must be led near grazing animals
Ordnance Survey maps	Landrangers 174 (Newbury & Wantage) and 185 (Winchester & Basingstoke), Explorer 144 (Basingstoke, Alton & Whitchurch)

GPS waypoints

- Start: SU 526 586
- A: SU 538 567
- B: SU 537 555
- C: SU 515 564
- D: SU 496 568
- E: SU 484 577
- F: SU 496 591
- G: SU 500 597
- H: SU 513 595
- J: SU 522 589

Just a few miles from Newbury, the attractive village of Kingsclere lies at the foot of the great chalk ridge that gazes out across the Berkshire border. From here, the walk climbs onto the Downs at Hannington before joining the long-distance Wayfarers' Walk along the top of the ridge. After dropping off the Downs past Sydmonton Court, home of the composer Andrew (now Baron) Lloyd-Webber, it makes its way to the tiny village of Ecchinswell before returning through the fields to Kingsclere.

Leave the car park and walk down Anchor Road towards the church; turn right into Swan Street, then right again into George Street, and walk up through the village. Fork right at **The George and Horn** pub, and almost immediately right again into The Dell. As the lane bears right, keep ahead along the signposted bridleway that climbs steadily to reward you with views to the television mast on Cottington's Hill. The track levels off, then drops briefly to a junction as another track trails in from your right.

A few paces farther on, turn right through a gap beside a metal field gate and continue along an exposed green track across the open fields with the television mast to your right. Soon the track bears left and climbs steadily past a stile and footpath turning on your right, to reach a junction by a large green fertiliser tank A.

Keep ahead here, following the hedge on your right through a shallow valley. At the top of the hill the track bends left, then right, and passes beneath electricity lines before reaching

Meadham Lane at a metal gate. Turn right for 50 yds, then turn off left just to the right of a wooden field gate and follow the green track beside the hedge on your left to a junction by a small pedestrian gate B.

Turn left here if you'd like to visit the pretty village of Hannington and the **Vine Inn**. Otherwise turn right, still with the boundary hedge on your left. Dodge around the metal gate in the far corner of the field and turn immediately right, now following the signposted footpath beside the hedge on your right until it returns to Meadham Lane at a pair of metal field gates.

Zigzag left and right across the lane, joining the signposted Wayfarers' Walk along an enclosed byway. Continue as the right-hand hedge drops away and the waymarked byway follows the wire fence on your left to reach a small parking area on the road at White Hill C.

Cross with care, dodging left and right to follow the Wayfarers' Walk (WW) along the gravelled track towards Inkpen Beacon. This is fast, easy walking along the top of the scarp slope with wide, far-reaching views.

After about a mile, you'll pass the end of a beech hanger – a long narrow belt of trees stretching down into the valley on your left.

Just beyond the beech hanger, follow the waymarked WW as it bears to the right D just before a concrete Ordnance Survey pillar and drops through a gate towards Sydmonton, now visible at the foot of the hill. Continue down the narrow path to the lane, cross over, and follow the WW through a gate onto a gravelled track fringed with beech trees on your right.

After 200 yds, turn right through a signposted wooden gate by an electricity pylon, leaving the WW and joining a grassy footpath. This sheltered path winds around the hillside, dropping gently through a sunken way and over a stile, then levelling out into a track that heads due north to a stile by the road at Sydmonton. Turn left along the road for 200 yds to a footpath signpost beside a bus stop E.

Turn right through a gate to follow the tree-lined path through the grounds of Sydmonton Court. Beyond the house itself, ignore all turnings as the path matures into a gravelled lane with clipped hedges on both sides. Follow this lane as it bends right, then left, towards the brick-built terrace of Laundry Cottages. Halfway to the cottages after the left-hand bend, turn right onto a similar lane that leads out between the buildings at Watership Farm to meet the lane at Ecchinswell F.

Turn left along the lane, pass the turning to Burghclere, and keep ahead through the village. Pass the **Royal Oak**, the turning to Kingsclere and the village school, then continue to the war memorial G.

Turn right here along the signposted footpath. For the first few paces it follows a track, then veers off left along a narrow path beside a small brook. Keep ahead when a path turns off to your right across the brook, and continue to a junction at a water pumping station. Turn right, cross the bridge, and continue with an open field across the brook on your right. Keep ahead as a footpath turns off to your left at a waymark post, and dive into Southwood Copse.

The path leaves the copse via a footbridge and continues along the woodland edge at the right-hand side of the next field. Cross the bridge at the corner of the field and follow the bridleway to the right when a path turns off to your left. The bridleway winds beside the light industrial buildings on your right and turns left onto the access road. Continue for about 100 yds to a bridleway and footpath marker post on your left Ⓗ.

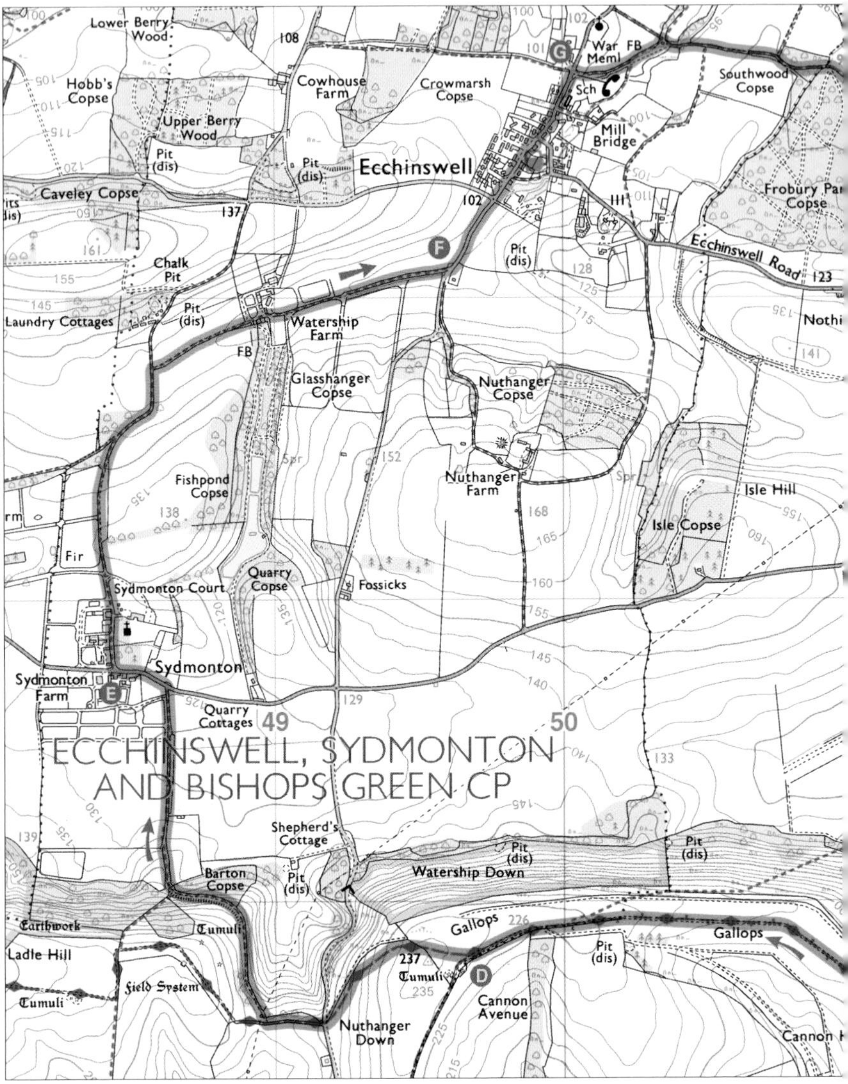

Fork left here, then bear around to the right, walking parallel with the road on the other side of the brook. Turn off to the left at the next yellow waymark arrow and walk along the edge of a field beside the hedge on your left. Zigzag right, then left around the barns at Porch Farm, still following the left-hand hedge to a stout waymark post in the corner of the field. Now bear right, and walk diagonally across the next field

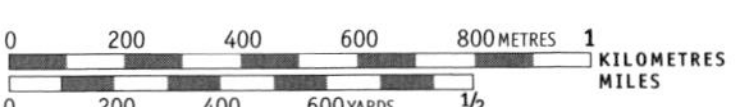

towards the far corner. Go through the pedestrian gate and continue along the enclosed path, which merges with a track to reach Kingsclere at the Newbury Road Ⓙ.

Cross over, turn right, and follow the road around to the left past the junction with Fox's Lane. Cross Cedar Drive and turn right at the church, then left into Anchor Road to return to your car. ●

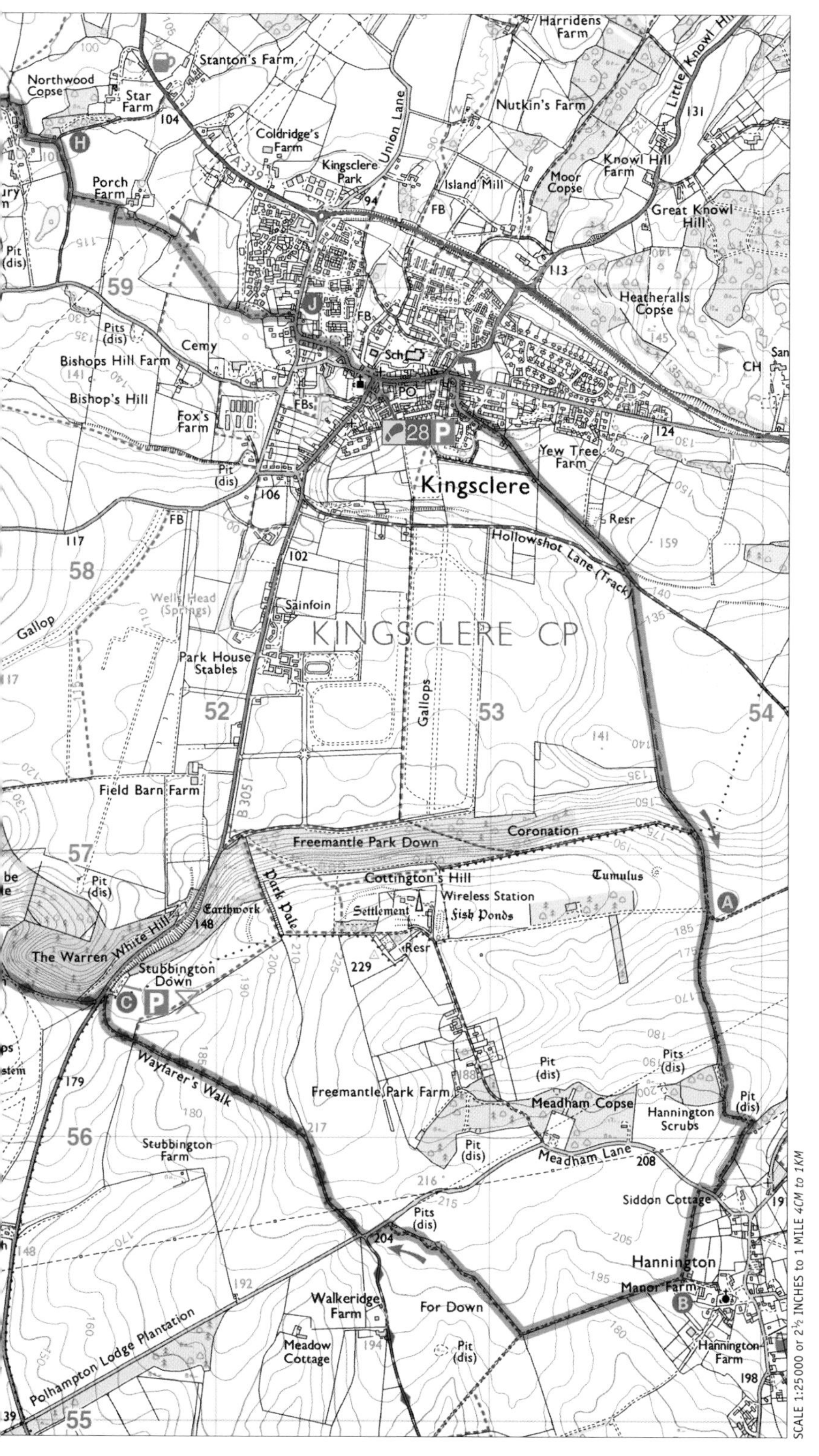
Harridens Farm
Stanton's Farm
Northwood Copse
Star Farm
Nutkin's Farm
Little Knowl Hill
Union Lane
Coldridge's Farm
Kingsclere Park
Island Mill
Porch Farm
Moor Copse
Knowl Hill Farm
Great Knowl Hill
Heatheralls Copse
Bishops Hill Farm
Bishop's Hill
Cemy
Fox's Farm
Yew Tree Farm
Kingsclere
Hollowshot Lane (Track)
Wells Head (Springs)
Sainfoin
KINGSCLERE CP
Park House Stables
Gallops
Gallop
Field Barn Farm
Freemantle Park Down
Coronation
Cottington's Hill
Wireless Station
Tumulus
Fish Ponds
Settlement
Earthwork
Park Pale
The Warren White Hill
Stubbington Down
Wayfarer's Walk
Freemantle Park Farm
Meadham Copse
Hannington Scrubs
Meadham Lane
Siddon Cottage
Stubbington Farm
Hannington
Manor Farm
Walkeridge Farm
For Down
Meadow Cottage
Hannington Farm
Polhampton Lodge Plantation
SCALE 1:25000 or 2½ INCHES to 1 MILE 4CM to 1KM

Further Information

Long-distance Paths

Hampshire County Council, who are responsible for all rights of way in the county, have established a system of special long-distance paths. These are distinctively signposted, waymarked and maintained to ensure that they are easy to follow. There are eight paths in all, criss-crossing the county, and they have been designed both to connect places of interest and to pass through beautiful countryside.

1 The Solent Way, 60 miles (96km), runs along the coast from Christchurch to Emsworth.
2 The Wayfarers' Walk, 70 miles (113km), goes diagonally north–south from Inkpen Beacon to near Portsmouth.
3 The South Downs Way, a national trail, is 90 miles (145km) long and runs east from Winchester to Eastbourne.
4 The Hangers Way, 17 miles (27km), follows the Hampshire Hangers, steep-sided hills that run north from Petersfield to Alton.
5 The Test Way, 46 miles (74km) long, runs mainly along the Test Valley from Totton to Inkpen Beacon.
6 The Clarendon Way, which is 24 miles (39km) in length, goes from Salisbury to Winchester.
7 The Staunton Way, 14 miles (22.5km), runs from Queen Elizabeth Country Park to Havant.
8 The Avon Valley Path is 34 miles (55km) long and follows the Avon valley from Salisbury to Christchurch.

Sections of many of these paths form part of routes in this book but, having done these walks, why not follow some of the long-distance routes either walking one complete route over a few days or doing just a short section at a time.

Hampshire County Councils' Countryside and Community Department have free leaflets on all the paths, except the Wayfarers' Walk on which there is a booklet. The leaflets are available from local tourist information centres and some libraries, or send a stamped addressed envelope to the address on page 94.

The Ramblers' Association

No organisation works more actively to protect and extend the rights and interests of walkers in the countryside than the Ramblers' Association. Its aims are clear: to foster a greater knowledge, love and care of the countryside; to assist in the protection and enhancement of public rights of way and areas of natural beauty; to work for greater public access to the countryside; and to encourage more people to take up rambling as a healthy, recreational leisure activity.

It was founded in 1935 when, following the setting up of a National Council of Ramblers' Federation in 1931, a number of federations in London, Manchester, the Midlands and elsewhere came together to create a more effective pressure group, to deal with such problems as the disappearance or obstruction of footpaths, the prevention of access to open mountain and moorland, and increasing hostility from landowners. This was the era of the mass trespasses, when there were sometimes violent confrontations between ramblers and gamekeepers, especially on the moorlands of the Peak District.

Since then the Ramblers' Association has played a key role in preserving and developing the national footpath network, supporting the creation of national parks and encouraging the designation and waymarking of long-distance routes.

Our freedom of access to the countryside, now enshrined in legislation, is still in its early years and requires constant vigilance. But over and above this there will always be the problem of footpaths being illegally obstructed, disappearing through lack of use, or being extinguished by housing or road construction.

It is to meet such problems and dangers that the Ramblers' Association exists and represents the interests of all walkers. The address to write to for information on the Ramblers' Association and how to become a member is given on page 95.

Walkers and the Law

The Countryside and Rights of Way Act (CRoW Act 2000) extends the rights of access previously enjoyed by walkers in England and Wales. Implementation of these rights began on 19 September 2004. The Act amends existing legislation and for the first time provides access on foot to certain types of land – defined as mountain, moor, heath, down and registered common land.

Where You Can Go

Rights of Way

Prior to the introduction of the CRoW Act, walkers could only legally access the countryside along public rights of way. These are either 'footpaths' (for walkers only) or 'bridleways' (for walkers, riders on horseback and pedal cyclists). A third category called 'Byways open to all traffic' (BOATs), is used by motorised vehicles as well as those using non-mechanised transport. Mainly they are green lanes, farm and estate roads, although occasionally they will be found crossing mountainous area.

Rights of way are marked on Ordnance Survey maps. Look for the green broken lines on the Explorer maps, or the red dashed lines on Landranger maps.

The term 'right of way' means exactly what it says. It gives a right of passage over what, for the most part, is private land. Under pre-CRoW legislation walkers were required to keep to the line of the right of way and not stray onto land on either side. If you did inadvertently wander off the right of way, either because of faulty map reading or because the route was not clearly indicated on the ground, you were technically trespassing.

Local authorities have a legal obligation to ensure that rights of way are kept clear and free of obstruction, and are signposted where they leave metalled roads. The duty of local authorities to install signposts extends to the placing of signs along a path or way, but only where the authority considers it necessary to have a signpost or waymark to assist persons unfamiliar with the locality.

The New Access Rights

Access Land

As well as being able to walk on existing rights of way, under the new legislation you now have access to large areas of open land. You can of course continue to use rights of way footpaths to cross this land, but the main difference is that you can now lawfully leave the path and wander at will, but only in areas designated as access land.

Where to Walk

Areas now covered by the new access rights – Access Land – are shown on Ordnance Survey Explorer maps bearing the access land symbol on the front cover.

'Access Land' is shown on Ordnance Survey maps by a light yellow tint surrounded by a pale orange border. New orange coloured 'i' symbols on the maps will show the location of permanent access information boards installed by the access authorities.

Restrictions

The right to walk on access land may lawfully be restricted by landowners. Landowners can, for any reason, restrict access for up to 28 days in any year. They cannot however close the land:

- on bank holidays;
- for more than four Saturdays and Sundays in a year;
- on any Saturday from 1 June to 11 August; or
- on any Sunday from 1 June to the end of September.

They have to provide local authorities with five working days' notice before the date of closure unless the land involved is an area of less than five hectares or the closure is for less than four hours. In these cases land-owners only need to provide two hours' notice.

Whatever restrictions are put into place on access land they have no effect on existing rights of way, and you can continue to walk on them.

Dogs

Dogs can be taken on access land, but must be kept on leads of two metres or less between 1 March and 31 July, and at all times where they are near livestock. In addition land-owners may impose a ban on all dogs from fields where lambing takes place for up to six weeks in any year. Dogs may be banned from moorland used for grouse shooting and breeding for up to five years.

In the main, walkers following the routes in this book will continue to follow existing rights of way, but a knowledge and understanding of the law as it affects walkers, plus the ability to distinguish access land marked on the maps, will enable anyone who wishes to depart from paths that cross access land either to take a shortcut, to enjoy a view or to explore.

General Obstructions

Obstructions can sometimes cause a problem on a walk and the most common of these is where the path across a field has been ploughed over. It is legal for a farmer to plough up a path provided that it is restored within two weeks. This does not always happen and you are faced with the dilemma of following the line of the path, even if this means treading on crops, or walking round the edge of the field. Although the latter course of action seems the most sensible, it does mean that you would be trespassing.

Other obstructions can vary from overhanging vegetation to wire fences across the path, locked gates or even a cattle feeder on the path.

Use common sense. If you can get round the obstruction without causing damage, do so. Otherwise only remove as much of the obstruction as is necessary to secure passage.

If the right of way is blocked and cannot be followed, there is a long-standing view that in such circumstances there is a right to deviate, but this cannot wholly be relied on. Although it is accepted in law that highways (and that includes rights of way) are for the public service, and if the usual track is impassable, it is for the general good that people should be entitled to pass into another line. However, this should not be taken as indicating a right to deviate whenever a way becomes impassable. If in doubt, retreat.

Report obstructions to the local authority and/or The Ramblers.

Useful Organisations

Campaign to Protect Rural England
128 Southwark Street,
London SE1 0SW
Tel. 020 7981 2800
www.cpre.org.uk

Forestry Commission
231 Corstorphine Road, Edinburgh
EH12 7AT
Tel. 0131 334 0303
www.forestry.gov.uk

Forest Enterprise, South East England Forest District, Bucks Horn Oak, Farnham, Surrey GU10 4LS
Tel. 01420 23666

Hampshire County Council
Rights of Way section, Countryside Service, Mottisfont Court, High Street, Winchester, SO23 8ZF
Tel. 0845 603 5636
www.hants.gov.uk

Hampshire & Isle of Wight Wildlife Trust
Beechcroft House, Vicarage Lane, Curdridge, Hampshire
SO32 2DP
Tel. 01489 774400
www.hwt.org.uk

Long Distance Walkers' Association
Bellevue, Princes Street, Ulverston, Cumbria
LA12 7NB
www.ldwa.org.uk

National Trust
Membership and general enquiries:
PO Box 39, Warrington
WA5 7WD
Tel. 0844 800 1895
www.nationaltrust.org.uk
Thames & Solent Office:
Hughenden Manor,
High Wycombe,
Bucks HP14 4LA
Tel. 01494 755500

Natural England
1 Southampton Road,
Lyndhurst, Hampshire
SO43 7BU
Tel. 0300 060 2514
www.naturalengland.gov.uk

Ordnance Survey
Romsey Road,
Southampton
SO16 4GU
Tel. 08456 05 05 05 (Lo-call)
www.ordnancesurvey.co.uk

Ramblers' Association
2nd Floor, Camelford House,
87–90 Albert Embankment,
London
SE1 7TW
Tel. 020 7339 8500
www.ramblers.org.uk

Tourism South East
40 Chamberlayne Road,
Eastleigh, Hampshire
SO50 5JH
Tel. 02380 625400
www.visitsoutheastengland.com

Local tourist information numbers:
Aldershot: 01252 320968
Andover: 01264 324320
Fareham: 01329 221342
Fordingbridge: 01425 654560
Gosport: 023 9252 2944
Hayling Island & Havant: 023 9246 7111
Lymington: 01590 689000
Lyndhurst and New Forest: 023 8028 2269
Petersfield: 01730 268829
Portsmouth, The Hard: 023 9282 6722
Ringwood: 01425 470896
Romsey: 01794 512987
Southampton: 023 8083 3333
Winchester: 01962 840500

Youth Hostels Association
Trevelyan House, Dimple Road,
Matlock, Derbyshire
DE4 3YH
Tel. 01629 592600
www.yha.org.uk

Ordnance Survey maps of Hampshire

Hampshire is covered by Ordnance Survey 1:50 000 scale (1¼ inches to 1 mile or 2cm to 1km) Landranger map sheets 184, 185, 186, 195, 196 and 197. These all-purpose maps are packed with information to help you explore the area. Viewpoints, picnic sites, places of interest and caravan and camping sites are shown, as well as public rights of way information such as footpaths and bridleways.

To examine Hampshire in more detail, and especially if you are planning walks, Ordnance Survey Explorer maps at 1:25 000 scale (4cm to 1km or 2½ inches to 1 mile) are ideal. Maps covering this area are:

119 (Meon Valley, Portsmouth, Gosport & Fareham)
120 (Chichester)
130 (Salisbury & Stonehenge)
131 (Romsey, Andover & Test Valley)
132 (Winchester)
133 (Haslemere & Petersfield)
144 (Basingstoke, Alton & Whitchurch)
158 (Newbury & Hungerford)
159 (Reading)

Explorer OL22 (New Forest) covers part of Hampshire and is also at 1:25 000 scale (2½ inches to 1 mile) scale.

To get to Hampshire, use the Ordnance Survey OS Travel Map-Road 8 (South East England) at 1:250 000 scale (1cm to 2.5km or 1 inch to 4 miles).

Ordnance Survey maps and guides are available from most booksellers, stationers and newsagents.

Further Information